NUCLEAR SUPERIORITY
The 'new triad' and the evolution of nuclear strategy

DAVID S. McDONOUGH

ADELPHI PAPER 383

The International Institute for Strategic Studies
Arundel House | 13–15 Arundel Street | Temple Place | London | WC2R 3DX | UK

ADELPHI PAPER 383

First published October 2006 by **Routledge**
4 Park Square, Milton Park, Abingdon, Oxon, OX14 4RN

for **The International Institute for Strategic Studies**
Arundel House, 13–15 Arundel Street, Temple Place, London, WC2R 3DX, UK
www.iiss.org

Simultaneously published in the USA and Canada by **Routledge**
711 Third Avenue, New York, NY 10017

Routledge is an imprint of Taylor & Francis, an Informa business

© 2006 The International Institute for Strategic Studies

DIRECTOR-GENERAL AND CHIEF EXECUTIVE John Chipman
EDITOR Tim Huxley
MANAGER FOR EDITORIAL SERVICES Ayse Abdullah
ASSISTANT EDITOR Jessica Delaney
PRODUCTION Jesse Simon
COVER IMAGE Stone Collection/Getty Images

All rights reserved. No part of this book may be reprinted or reproduced or utilised in any form or by any electronic, mechanical, or other means, now known or hereafter invented, including photocopying and recording, or in any information storage or retrieval system, without permission in writing from the publisher.

British Library Cataloguing in Publication Data
A catalogue record for this book is available from the British Library

Library of Congress Cataloguing in Publication Data

ISBN 978-0-415-42734-0
ISSN 0567-932X

Contents

GLOSSARY

ABL	Airborne Laser
ABM	Anti-ballistic missile
ABMDS	*Aegis* Ballistic Missile Defense System
ACI	Advanced Concepts Initiative
ACM	Advanced cruise missile
ADW	Agent-defeat weapons
AFSP	Air Force Space Command
ALCM	Air-launched cruise missile
BMD	Ballistic-missile defence
BMDO	Ballistic Missile Defense Organization
BUR	Bottom-Up Review
C^2I	Command, control and intelligence
C^3	Command, control and communications
CB	Chemical and biological
CEP	Circular error probable
CONPLAN	Concept Plan
CRS	Congressional Research Service
CTM	Conventional *Trident* Modification
DCI	Defense Counterproliferation Initiative
DGZ	Designated Ground Zero
DoD	Department of Defense
DPG	Defense Planning Guidance
EPW	Earth-penetrator weapons
GBI	Ground-based interceptors
GMD	Ground-based Midcourse Defence
GPALS	Global Protection Against Limited Strikes
HDBT	Hardened and deeply buried target
ICBM	Intercontinental ballistic missile
ISR	Intelligence, surveillance and reconnaissance
JCS	Joint Chiefs of Staff
JSCP	Joint Strategic Capabilities Plan
JSOP	Joint Strategic Objectives Plan
LEP	Life Extension Program
LOW	Launch-on-warning
LUA	Launch-under-attack
MAD	Mutual assured deterrence
MARV	Manoeuvrable re-entry vehicle
MEADS	Medium Extended Air Defense System

MIRV	Multiple independently targetable re-entry vehicle
MPF	Modern Pit Facility
MRBM	Medium-range ballistic missile
MRC	Major regional conflict
MRT	Mobile and relocatable targets
MX	Missile-experimental
NBC	Nuclear, biological and chemical
NIE	National Intelligence Estimate
NMD	National missile defence
NNSA	National Nuclear Security Administration
NPR	*Nuclear Posture Review*
NPT	Non-Proliferation Treaty
NSC	National Security Council
NSDM	National Security Decision Memorandum
NSPD	National Security Presidential Directive
NSS	National Security Strategy
NTS	Nevada Test Site
NTW	Navy Theater Wide
NUWEP	Nuclear Weapons Employment Policy
NWC	Nuclear Weapons Council
NWPTF	Nuclear Weapons Project Task Force
OPLAN	Operations Plan
PAC	*Patriot* Advanced Capability
PDD	Presidential Decision Directive
PLYWD	Precision Low-Yield Weapons Design
QDR	*Quadrennial Defense Review*
RNEP	Robust Nuclear Earth Penetrator
RRW	Reliable Replacement Warhead
RV	Re-entry vehicle
SAC	Strategic Air Command
SAM	Surface-to-air missile
SBL	Space-based Laser
SDI	Strategic Defense Initiative
SIOP	Single Integrated Operations Plan
SLBM	Sea-launched ballistic missile
SMD	Sea-based Midcourse Defense
SORT	Strategic Offensive Reduction Treaty
SSBN	Ballistic-missile submarine
SSP	Stockpile Stewardship Program
STRATCOM	Strategic Command
STSS	Space Tracking and Surveillance System
SWPS	Strategic War-Planning System
THAAD	Theater High Altitude Area Defense
TMD	Theatre missile defence
USAF	United States Air Force
WMD	Weapons of mass destruction

INTRODUCTION

The administration of George W. Bush has attempted to implement a number of significant revisions to American nuclear strategy. Perhaps the most controversial has been the proposal for new nuclear capabilities designed for *specialised* counter-force missions against hardened underground bunkers, weapons of mass destruction (WMD) and other strategic military 'assets'. Many are found among those regional adversaries that have been colloquially termed 'rogue states' – and perhaps better called states with rogue regimes – and, not surprisingly, these states have been incorporated as critical targets in the increasingly prompt and flexible US nuclear-war plans. These nuclear-weapon proposals have faced criticism from many quarters and many specific recommendations have been defeated in Congress. Yet it remains to be seen whether the 'transformation' of the American nuclear arsenal has indeed stalled in the long term. After all, the military utility of using nuclear 'bunker-busters' as a tool of 'counter-proliferation', ostensibly to make more credible American efforts to reinforce deterrence, has become the new *raison d'être* for the nuclear arsenal. The wisdom of adopting such a rationale, which appears to ignore the existential threats posed by the large arsenal of Russian and other nuclear stockpiles, can, therefore, be brought into question.

But the current process of nuclear transformation goes beyond the dream of bunker-busters, expanded targeting options and other forms of nuclear counter-force modernisation; it threatens to contribute to the notion that nuclear weapons can be equated with conventional weapons. The late

Hans Morgenthau aptly termed such a characterisation the 'conventionalisation' of nuclear weapons. A less noticed but equally important chapter of this story is the continuing modernisation of the traditional 'nuclear triad', consisting of intercontinental ballistic missiles (ICBMs), sea-launched ballistic missiles (SLBMs) and a fleet of nuclear-armed intercontinental bombers. Indeed, the modernisation of the traditional strategic arsenal will not only give these 'legacy nuclear systems' an extended service life, but will also significantly expand the 'hard-target-kill' capabilities of these systems against a number of traditional counter-force targets – not only among regional adversaries or nascent nuclear powers, but more importantly, against such established (and potentially rival) major powers as Russia and China. Strategic force modernisation is taking place in the context of force reductions, based on the US–Russian agreement in the Moscow Treaty on Strategic Offensive Reductions (SORT) of May 2002. It is, however, questionable whether these reductions will indeed result in strategic nuclear stability, given the ongoing drive for qualitative improvements in the American nuclear arsenal.

The controversy surrounding many of these developments originated in the 2002 *Nuclear Posture Review* (NPR). This document, mandated by the Defense Authorization Act for Fiscal Year 2001, was finally submitted to Congress on 8 January 2002. The 2002 NPR outlines a 'new triad' concept to replace the traditional nuclear triad rationale for the American strategic force posture. The traditional strategic arsenal of ICBMs, SLBMs and penetrating bombers would be combined with conventional strike capabilities to form the 'offensive strike systems' leg of the new triad. The second leg would consist of defences, most notably such active 'damage-limiting' measures as the US plan to field a multi-layered ballistic-missile defence (BMD) system. The third leg of the new triad concept would consist of a revitalised defence infrastructure that would be more responsive to developing new capabilities (nuclear and non-nuclear) if required.[1]

In the post-Cold War period, while US administrations have struggled to develop a compelling narrative to justify the residual role of nuclear weapons from the Cold War, the need for proactive counter-proliferation measures appears to have become the primary de facto rationale for US post-Cold War nuclear-weapon developments.[2] Counter-proliferation originated early in the post-Cold War period, as a result of the seemingly inevitable 'horizontal' challenge of WMD proliferation that was forcefully communicated to American defence planners during the 1990–91 Gulf War and the 1994 North Korean nuclear crisis. As a result, the US began to focus not only on developing means of preventing the spread of such exotic weapons, typically through a *mélange* of unilateral, bilateral and multilateral non-proliferation measures, but also on more assertive ways of dealing with the strategic and military results of proliferation – including preparation to fight and win wars in a WMD environment. This signalled a growing American suspicion of the utility of traditional multilateral non-proliferation solutions, and the gradual acceptance that unilateral measures were now a necessary (if not sufficient) component for preventing and/or containing the threat of WMD proliferation.

The new triad strategy intersects with and subsumes two inter-related developments of this post-Cold War trend. The first is the growth of counter-proliferation as an integral component of US nuclear-targeting policy. American nuclear-war planners were quick to incorporate rogue states and their suspected WMD capabilities as key nuclear-targeting options in the 1990s. This even led to early nuclear initiatives spearheaded by the National Nuclear Security Administration (NNSA), which was keen to reinvigorate a largely moribund warhead-design community, in order to develop specialised nuclear warheads specifically tailored for counter-proliferation missions. The second development has been called the third American debate on ballistic missile defence. While the first and second debates took place during the Cold War in the context of the nuclear threat posed by the Soviet Union, the third debate differs from the first two in terms of the case it has made for BMD, which, in its emphasis on horizontal WMD proliferation, is firmly rooted in the need for counter-proliferation.[3] Missile defences may play a role in deterring the development of ballistic missiles, but they could also provide a very useful damage-limiting safety net in any counter-force and counter-proliferation mission.

The Bush administration's modifications to US nuclear strategy constitute the latest manifestation of a long-standing trend towards maintaining and expanding America's nuclear superiority by the accelerated development of counter-force capabilities. This entails the need to reinforce US capabilities to target an adversary's strategic forces, in order to bolster the credibility of the nuclear deterrent and, perhaps more importantly, to prepare for nuclear use in the event of its failure. This view is founded on the idea of 'deterrence by denial', whereby the emphasis is placed squarely on counter-force capabilities, including offensive strike and active defence, that would deny or eliminate the value of an adversary's own deterrent. Such a posture would, according to this logic, deter an adversary from aggression, given the surety that the United States would have a wide range of capabilities to deny the adversary's objectives. As noted by Robert Jervis, 'Deterrence by denial means deterring the adversary by convincing him that any attack will be thwarted, that he cannot win.'[4] This is much more ambitious than a 'deterrence-by-punishment' strategy that only advocates sufficient nuclear capabilities to punish an aggressor. As severe and catastrophic as the punishment may be, it would at least allow an adversary to maintain its own capability for a reciprocal punishing deterrent. Retaliatory punishment is highly conducive to a situation of 'mutual assured deterrence' (MAD), while deterrence by denial places a premium on a credible and robust ability to deny the adversary's own deterrent capability. MAD would be replaced with the 'unilateral assured destruction' of an adversary's nuclear assets for the purposes of deterrence.

The concept of denial which underpins the new triad strategy represents the latest move towards attaining the elusive ability to control and dominate the escalatory process of conflict. This has been a long-standing goal for proponents of nuclear-counter-force capabilities, many of whom witnessed the arrival of mutual deterrence – and the American constraints implicit in such a MAD arrangement – with varying degrees of apprehension.[5] The way out of this situation was a redefinition of deterrence that entailed a form of nuclear superiority over prospective adversaries. The fact that Russia lacks the resources to maintain and operate sufficient nuclear forces to maintain a semblance of strategic parity, and other potential nuclear adversaries have even more significant hurdles to overcome in attaining a survivable (let alone significant) nuclear arsenal, has only reinforced the feasibility of managing America's nuclear legacy by extending its counter-force superiority. 'Escalation dominance' may ultimately allow for more credible nuclear threats and a more robust deterrent posture, but it would also be a necessary step for more ambitious coercive strategies (e.g. compellence) and would form the basis for controlling strategies (e.g. 'satisfactory war termination') in the event of deterrence failure or efforts to roll back the WMD capabilities of regional adversaries.[6]

The expansion of American counter-force capabilities was especially prominent in the latter years of the Cold War, and can be seen in the 'countervailing' and 'prevailing' strategies of the Jimmy Carter and Ronald Reagan administrations respectively. The new triad strategy, however, has coalesced in a remarkably different strategic environment. The context for the most recent evolutionary phase is no longer bipolarity, where escalation dominance was meant to deter an adversary that had gradually achieved strategic parity with the United States. Instead, it has taken place in an environment of American unipolarity and drive towards grand strategic primacy, where the immediate threats are posed by strategically weak and highly asymmetrical regional adversaries that are more likely to be armed with chemical and biological (CB) weapons than a significant nuclear arsenal, and where even potential 'near-peer competitors' represent but a pale shadow of the Soviet threat. It is true that various components of the new triad, from its emphasis on BMD to its advocacy of non-nuclear strike systems, do represent a significant US effort to reduce reliance on nuclear forces. Yet the United States has also complemented these efforts with an attendant concern to improve the qualitative counter-force capability of its nuclear arsenal. The fact that these efforts have faced Congressional funding hurdles reveals the difficulty and controversy of initiating successful nuclear-warhead or nuclear-infrastructure modernisation proposals, but it does not lessen the importance of such force-modernisation proposals in the first place.

The new triad represents a complex and potentially contradictory effort to reduce American self-deterrence by de-emphasising the role of nuclear weapons through an expansion of non-nuclear components in US deterrence calculus, while simultaneously attempting to modify American nuclear forces to play a more tailored deterrent role against potential adversaries. 'Nuclear superiority' may be a long-standing goal of American nuclear-war planners, but the current strategic environment – defined by unprecedented American strategic power and potential adversaries with diverse sets of capabilities – has certainly altered the modalities of such a superiority. On the one hand, the sheer disparity in strategic capabilities between the United States and its regional adversaries magnifies the implicit idea of superiority inherent in escalation dominance. Rather than simply attaining sufficient levels of deterrence, current efforts at maintaining nuclear superiority would entail enabling military interventions and regime-change campaigns that might not have been possible against adversaries armed with more significant WMD capabilities. On the other hand, current strategic force-modernisation programmes could also provide a first-strike capability against potential major nuclear-weapon powers. While not enabling interventionism, the threat of a hypothetical disarming attack could constitute a useful leverage or bargaining advantage during any future crisis scenarios with these powers.

The strategic implications of the new triad strategy are enormous. It could strengthen the United States' ability to deal unilaterally with the threat posed by WMD, while giving the US greater freedom to use nuclear threats and other forms of coercion during a crisis with a potential peer competitor. The objective is bold: the 'prevention' of MAD from taking root with regional adversaries and its 'rollback' in US relations with established nuclear powers. This would in effect represent a return to the mythical 'golden age' of American nuclear superiority in the 1950s.[7] The consequences of nuclear superiority, irrespective of whether this vision is deliberate, are still uncertain, but one should not casually dismiss the potential temptation for unilateral military adventurism in support of counter-proliferation and WMD termination. Nor can one simply ignore the potential for strategic nuclear instability, and indeed a return to brandishing these weapons explicitly for political gains. The potential consequences of this strategy may be as far reaching as the strategy is ambitious.

This paper provides a historical context for the current administration's modifications to US nuclear strategy. It explains how the new triad strategy is founded on previous American efforts to secure both nuclear superiority against the Soviet Union and war-fighting, counter-proliferation capabilities against WMD-proliferant adversaries. It illustrates how the evolution of American nuclear strategy towards more effective and credible counter-force capabilities, rather than dissipating in the current strategic threat environment, has led to a host of counter-force developments, including renewed emphasis on nuclear targeting of non-nuclear states, prompt and flexible nuclear-war planning, and ongoing (if unsuccessful) efforts to develop specialised nuclear warheads and a modernised nuclear infrastructure that is responsive to these strategic developments. The strategic consequences of the current vision of nuclear transformation are examined, with particular emphasis on the likelihood of crisis instability with regional adversaries and renewed geostrategic competition, with the potential for strategic nuclear instability among established nuclear powers. It concludes with a proposal for a more limited counter-force approach, which could maximise the strategic advantages accrued from the new triad strategy and minimise the potential for strategic instability with both Russia and China.

CHAPTER ONE

The Evolution of American Nuclear Strategy[1]

The nuclear strategy of the United States was born in the aftermath of the decision to drop atomic bombs on Hiroshima and Nagasaki at the end of the Second World War. Initial recommendations may have highlighted the tactical potential of nuclear weapons to support a military invasion, but their use clearly followed the principles of strategic bombardment, insofar as the attacks were meant to coerce Japan to surrender, with the threat of further nuclear deployment in the event of non-compliance, rather than merely to support a conventional operation.[2] It was at this point that the United States began to formulate a coherent nuclear strategy, which was a lengthy endeavour owing to the unprecedented destructive capabilities inherent in atomic-fission and later thermonuclear-fusion weapons. Debate over the tactical utility of these weapons continued into the 1950s and 1960s, but a growing consensus gradually emerged that the sheer destructive power of these weapons made their use problematic in all but the most extreme situations. This may indeed have resulted in the much-celebrated 'taboo' over nuclear use that has persisted for over six decades.[3] But the *threat* of using these strategic weapons, alongside the nuclear targeting and war planning that made this threat a reality, did become an integral part of American policy.

The evolution of American nuclear strategy during the Cold War provides an important historical context for the changing nature of its nuclear strategy after the Cold War and, more specifically, for the debate over the Bush administration's more recent nuclear revisions. A common misconception of those who deride the Bush administration's strategy is that it represents a sharp, even revolutionary, departure from the prevailing consensus of MAD. From that perspective, the new triad strategy and its strong emphasis on counter-force targeting of non-nuclear adversaries, for strategic and potentially tactical purposes, could thereby be contrasted with the posture of retaliatory second-strike forces and nuclear counter-value weapons that are designed to destroy cities, population centres and other societal targets. However, the Cold War consensus on mutual deterrence was neither monolithic nor totally distinct from the 'war-fighting' strategy espoused by the Bush administration. Prior to the Soviet attainment of parity in nuclear weapons, when the strategic relationship between both powers was still highly asymmetrical, the US was able both to define deterrence as being based on American nuclear superiority and to consider a greater variety of options in dealing with the Soviet threat. With the Soviet development of a 'minimum nuclear deterrent', and the gradual emergence of 'nuclear parity' and 'strategic equivalence', deterrence began to be defined as *mutual* deterrence based on assured destruction, a concept that was both frightening in its uncertain implications for global stability and foreign to any previous US understanding. Questions about the nature of mutual deterrence would, however, continue to trouble policymakers. Some saw MAD as a situational fact arising from the mutual capability of each side to destroy the other, but others would argue that MAD was a defeatist doctrine that the US had mistakenly accepted and should, therefore, be challenged. Beginning in the 1970s and 1980s, the United States attempted to escape from the implications of nuclear parity and to reappraise the definition of deterrence to imply some level of superiority. This phase in the evolution of US nuclear strategy did *not* end with the demise of the Soviet Union, and indeed as an attendant consequence would be brought into sharper focus.

Nuclear monopoly, nuclear ambiguity

The administration of Harry Truman, despite its wartime decision to coerce Japan's surrender through atomic bombardment, was initially quite hesitant about the political and military utility of nuclear weapons. Nuclear weapons were viewed as weapons of terror rather than part of the conventional military arsenal. 'You got to understand', Truman told his advisers in 1946, 'that this isn't a military weapon. It is used to wipe out women and children and unarmed people, and not for military uses. So we have got to treat this differently from rifles and cannons and ordinary things like that.'[4]

This may have been the much-vaunted period of US nuclear monopoly, but the value of such a monopoly could certainly be questioned.

The number of atomic weapons and delivery systems was simply too few. This was noted immediately after the end of the Second World War in the 'Spaatz report', which determined that the scarcity of atomic bombs and the limited number and range of B-29 bombers made the use of these weapons unfeasible. These problems would remain constant for much of the duration of the Truman administration: 'There were only two weapons in the stockpile at the end of 1945, nine in July 1946, and fifty in July 1948.'[5] That being said, the administration did initiate nuclear-war plans emphasising strategic nuclear bombardment to neutralise 'the vital war-making capacity' of the Soviet Union.[6] Truman would also threaten to deploy nuclear weapons on two occasions, the 1948 Berlin crisis and the 1950–52 period of the Korean War, though these threats were ambiguous and hesitant.[7]

Perhaps more importantly, it was under this administration that the framework for subsequent US nuclear strategy would be formulated. In 1948, the National Security Council (NSC) approved NSC-30 on *United States Policy on Atomic Weapons*, which stated that the 'National Military Establishment must be ready to utilize promptly and effectively all appropriate means available, including atomic weapons, in the interest of national security and must therefore plan accordingly'.[8] In 1952, nuclear-war planning was institutionalised: the Joint Strategic Capabilities Plan (JSCP) governed wartime operations for the fiscal year; the Joint Strategic Objectives Plan (JSOP) governed force requirements for the next three to five years; and the Joint Long Range Strategic Estimate governed research and development requirements past the five-year JSOP plan. These plans, which were to form the basis of the first Single Integrated Operations Plan (SIOP) in 1960, advocated the use of nuclear weapons only as an option of last resort. The Truman administration also approved steps that would lead to the production of tactical nuclear weapons and thermonuclear 'super bombs'.[9] Non-nuclear components of nuclear weapons (bomb casings or assemblies) were forward deployed to Britain and French Morocco, while nuclear components and later nuclear capsules were deployed to Guam.[10] A conventional military approach may have been the key pillar of this administration's containment strategy, as clearly illustrated in the seminal NSC-68 document on *United States Objectives and Programs for National Security*, but it seems fair to say that the United States was at least hedging on the potential usability of nuclear weapons.

Many of these decisions stemmed from the perceived inevitability of the development of a Soviet nuclear arsenal. NSC-68 raised the spectre of the year of 'maximum danger', when it was estimated that the Soviet Union would have 200 nuclear bombs and could thereby seriously damage the United States. As the document notes, 'The existence of two large atomic capabilities in such a relationship might well act ... as an incitement for war.'[11] As pointed out by Marc Tratchenberg, the spectre of a Soviet nuclear arsenal had initiated a whole host of questions regarding the feasibility of a preventive war:

> If they were so hostile and aggressive even in the period of America's nuclear monopoly, what would they be like once this monopoly had been broken? There was no reason to assume that a nuclear world would be stable; wouldn't the Soviets some day try to destroy the one power that prevented them from achieving their goals by launching a nuclear attack on the United States? ...Wasn't some sort of more 'positive' policy worth considering?[12]

American defence planners would generate numerous reports and plans for such a 'positive' policy of preventive war under the Truman administration. Notwithstanding Truman's own reluctance to contemplate nuclear use, and the limited number of atomic bombs in the arsenal, these plans would explicitly feature conventional *and* nuclear weapons as integral war-fighting tools to destroy the Soviet military and industrial capabilities. The memory of the successful use of atomic weapons in the Second World War was, at this point in time, very fresh in the minds of American military leaders. NSC-68 would reject the option of preventive war and instead advocate an ambitious 'policy of calculated and gradual coercion' that would 'roll back the Kremlin's drive for world domination'. As Paul H. Nitze later noted, this would 'lay the basis for taking increased risks of general war in achieving a satisfactory solution of our relations with the USSR while her stockpile of atomic weapons was still small'.[13] As the year of maximum danger approached, more open deliberation on the merits of preventive war would arise once again to trouble the next administration.

The 'new look', massive retaliation and overkill

The Soviet Union tested its first nuclear bomb in 1949 and, with this one act, the remarkably short period of American nuclear monopoly came to an abrupt end. The event may have taken place under Truman's anxious watch, but it was to be under Dwight Eisenhower that the United States would have to deal with its full implications. The Eisenhower administration, and particularly Secretary of State John Foster Dulles, had a particularly alarmist view of the Soviet Union as an aggressive ideological adversary that sought to overthrow the existing order through subversion and limited war. The gradual development of a rudimentary nuclear capability, and its inevitable vertical proliferation, was seen to create a slowly shrinking window of nuclear superiority for the United States that would only abet the Soviets' aggressive regional designs.

Rather than posing a conventional and thereby symmetrical challenge, Eisenhower announced an asymmetrical 'new look' strategy that would rely on reacting to an adversary's challenges by applying one's strength against the other side's weakness.[14] The 'massive retaliation' doctrine was the key to this asymmetrical approach and would be enshrined in NSC-162/2 on *Basic National Security Policy*. As this document noted, the United States had 'manifest determination' to 'use its atomic capability and massive retaliatory striking power' to deter a Soviet attack on Europe.[15] Deterrence was defined as the capability to deter the Soviet Union through nuclear superiority. As Lawrence Freedman makes clear:

> It must be remembered that it had been felt originally that deterrence depended on an *imbalance* of terror in the West's favour. It was the preponderance of US nuclear forces, enhanced by the dynamism of her technology, that would keep the Soviet Union's expansive tendencies in check.[16]

American defence planners would wait for the seemingly inevitable Soviet acquisition of a nuclear arsenal with some alarm. Not surprisingly, preventive war options would, once again, come to the fore. In a 1953 memorandum to Dulles, Eisenhower noted that when the Soviets acquired thermonuclear weapons, the US might find itself vulnerable to a crippling strike. According to Eisenhower, 'in such circumstances, we would be forced to consider whether or not our duty to future generations did not require us to initiate war at the most propitious moment we could designate'.[17] The benefits of 'deliberately precipitating war' would be reiterated in a May 1954 Advance Study Group report by the Joint Chiefs of Staff (JCS). The preventive war option would only be ruled out in an updated *Basic National Security Policy* paper in the autumn of 1954 (though Soviet capabilities would continue to be seen in a very alarmist light, as clearly shown in the 'bomber gap' and 'missile gap' of the late 1950s). Yet the strategic logic of preventive war, based on the wisdom of attacking an adversary prior to its acquisition of a truly threatening strategic capability, would periodically surface again in relation to proliferant or threshold WMD adversaries. Indeed, it would form the basis for the Bush administration's pre-emptive (more accurately, preventive war) doctrine and would be highlighted in the 2003 counter-proliferation campaign against Iraq.

Massive retaliation was not simply rhetorical. It was explicitly brandished as a policy tool on at least six occasions by the United States. The 1954–55 Quemoy and Matsu crisis is particularly interesting, insofar as it appears that Eisenhower's private deliberations on nuclear use were more concrete than the administration's declaratory doctrine.[18] While seeking to use American nuclear superiority to undertake 'nuclear blackmail', many of these deliberations took place at a time when Soviet nuclear capabilities were significant enough to damage US territory seriously.[19]

The actual policies on nuclear weapons implemented by the Eisenhower administration largely corresponded to the massive retaliation doctrine. The nuclear-weapons stockpile, which numbered a modest 1,000 weapons in 1953, would eventually reach 18,000 by the end of the Eisenhower administration. Indeed, between 1958 and 1960 alone, the US nuclear stockpile tripled in size (from 6,000 to 18,000 warheads).[20] NSC-162/2 had laid out three priorities that were reflected in the 1953 approval of a three-year defence programme: offensive striking power, tactical nuclear weapons and strategic defence capabilities. Strategic Air Command (SAC), which had significant authority over the American nuclear arsenal, would receive a large portion of these appropriations. Nuclear-armed bombers would also be joined by an increasing array of ballistic-missile delivery systems, including the *Minuteman* ICBM and the *Polaris* SLBM. Smaller tactical nuclear weapons, designated to support conventional forces, were emphasised and would subsequently be deployed to various countries, primarily in Europe and East Asia, under the 'neither confirm nor deny' policy.[21] This would be complemented by a trend towards the greater miniaturisation of nuclear weapons, with the 4.5-tonne implosion fission bomb replaced by bombs weighing 0.45 and 1.36 tonnes. In order to protect American nuclear capabilities (as well as to provide some limited protection for its population), continental defence measures – such as early-warning radar networks, interceptor squadrons and surface-to-air missile (SAM) batteries – were initiated.

The war plans created by SAC featured elements of both nuclear overkill and pre-emption. Overkill refers to the excessive nature of the planned nuclear attack. According to the first SIOP, designated SIOP-62, a nuclear attack would consist of launching the entire operationally deployed strategic force of 3,500 nuclear weapons against 1,050 Designated Ground Zeroes (DGZs) in the Soviet Union, Communist China and satellite nations. This plan blurred the type of targets to be attacked, incorporated features of both counter-force and counter-value targeting, and lacked any strategic objectives.[22] While an effort was made to reduce the number of DGZs and to incorporate military objectives in nuclear targeting, nuclear overkill would only be significantly alterered with the demise of the Soviet Union and the attendant reduction in Russian targets. Even then, overkill would still be reflected in nuclear-war plans that emphasised the targeting of industrial and socio-economic 'war-supporting' facilities and the proliferation of targets in the Third World. A simultaneous emphasis was also placed on an American pre-emptive nuclear attack in the event of an imminent strike by an adversary. Eisenhower's top-secret review of 'US Policy in the Event of War', approved by the NSC in March 1959, 'appears to have kept the option of preemptive response to an impending Soviet strike'.[23] Pre-emption would not only remain a feature of the SIOP for the duration of the Cold War, but would in fact be reflected in both the residual post-Cold War emphasis on high-alert levels and preparation to launch-on-warning (LOW) of an impending attack, alongside planning for more limited pre-emptive strikes against regional proliferators.

From flexible response to mutual deterrence

Despite the alarm over the year of maximum danger, and the subsequent fears over Soviet strategic capabilities, it was the administration of John F. Kennedy that had to deal realistically with a substantial Soviet nuclear capability and attendant American vulnerability. Both the Kennedy and Lyndon Johnson administrations would rely on a 'flexible response' strategy that would decrease reliance on nuclear weapons to deter limited aggression and focus instead on the need to boost conventional capabilities, with clear reference to contingencies surrounding Berlin. This led to *Poodle Blanket*, a plan which laid out four phases of graduated response to Soviet provocations towards Berlin, of which only the fourth phase included the use of nuclear weapons. This plan would be approved as National Security Action Memorandum 109 in October 1961.[24]

The flexible-response strategy may have become best known for its conventional emphasis, but it also advocated more flexible and credible nuclear options to replace the pre-planned massive-retaliation response enshrined in SIOP-62. The dissatisfaction with massive retaliation and the overkill targeting of SIOP-62 could be seen during a high-level review of American nuclear options during the 1961 Berlin Crisis, in which Special Assistant for National Security Affairs George McBundy reported to Kennedy that SIOP-62 'calls for shooting off everything we have in one shot, and is so constructed as to make any more flexible course very difficult'.[25] As a result, the nuclear arsenal was expanded in an apparent effort to make nuclear deterrence more credible and nuclear war, if it indeed took place, more limited. An expansion of strategic and tactical nuclear-weapon deployments to the Pacific was initiated in order to deal with the Soviet Union, China and communist insurgent movements in Southeast Asia. By mid-1964, the number of nuclear weapons available was increased by 150%, while the number of *Polaris* and *Minuteman* SLBMs and ICBMs increased to 29 and 800 respectively. Indeed, the actual result of the flexible-response strategy was to create a significant US nuclear advantage. With the Soviet Union armed with only 30 ICBMs at the end of 1962, 'a counterforce strike by the United States in the early 1960s could perhaps have fully disarmed the Soviet Union'.[26]

The need for 'flexibility' led the Kennedy administration to look at ways to expand and restructure the nuclear-targeting options codified in SIOP-62. Rather than being limited to the option of launching the entire nuclear arsenal against all the Communist Bloc countries, the administration argued for flexible and selective nuclear options against a range of different targets. This argument would, however, fall on deaf ears at a Pentagon still enamoured with the deliberative overkill SIOP plan, and it would be left to successive administrations to realise fully this type of targeting policy. Indeed, current American efforts to attain an even more rapid and flexible nuclear-war-planning capability, for both anticipated and unexpected scenarios, can be seen as the latest – and the most sophisticated – expression of targeting policy that originated in Kennedy's fascination with flexible response.

The administration was more successful, however, in advocating the strategic utility of counter-force attacks, ostensibly to achieve flexible nuclear options, but in fact to obtain a pre-emptive first-strike capability.[27] Out of the Soviet Bloc Target List for June 1969, only 11.3% of 1,860 Soviet-bloc targets were urban-industrial, the rest being nuclear-delivery systems, SAM sites and aircraft bases, command-and-control centres, and WMD-production and storage facilities. The flexible-response strategy, therefore, led to a nuclear-targeting policy that leaned heavily towards the idea of 'no cities' or 'city avoidance', whereby these targets would serve as useful 'withhold' options for intrawar deterrence in the event of nuclear war. As Secretary of Defense Robert McNamara pointed out in June 1962, the 'principal military objectives, in the event of a nuclear war … should be the destruction of the enemy's military forces, not of his civilian population'.[28]

Not surprisingly, the American emphasis on creating options for 'no-cities' counter-force attacks against Soviet nuclear and conventional forces elicited a hostile reaction from the Soviet Union. Not only was it in an inferior nuclear position and vulnerable to an American first strike, but the United States Air Force (USAF) also seemed to be heavily enamoured with the idea of 'strategic superiority', to the extent that counter-force was associated with the 'capacity to fight and win a nuclear war'. As Freedman would later add, USAF officers justified expensive new programmes under the 'counter-force' label and 'spoke and wrote about nuclear war, as a normal military operation rather than as a hideous eventuality, involving deep horror and tragedy'.[29]

Owing partly to both the adverse Soviet reaction and the knowledge that the destruction of missiles would become unfeasible as the Soviet arsenal gradually expanded, MAD eventually replaced 'city avoidance'. This doctrine refers to American and, more controversially, Soviet attainment of assured-destruction capability – the ability to deter an attack through the capacity to absorb a first strike while retaining the ability to inflict unacceptable damage in retaliation. The unacceptable degree of destruction commonly cited was 20–33% of an adversary's population and 50–75% of its industrial capacity. This concept represented a sharp departure from ideas prevalent in the 1950s when deterrence was based on the idea of US nuclear superiority and where parity was a danger best avoided, lest a 'delicate balance of terror' be created. With the acceptance of MAD, Soviet nuclear capabilities began to be seen in a more positive and reassuring light – the balance of terror was 'stable' rather than 'fragile'. However, it was only after 1967 that the declaratory doctrine of the United States was dominated by talk of assured destruction and MAD, and, even then, actual policy remained focused on a mix of counter-value and counter-force targeting. For example, the February 1967 JSOP continued to stress 'such notions as options, control, flexibility, and sequential attacks'.[30] A disjunction was, therefore, created between doctrine and operational policy under the Kennedy administration that would continue to plague its Cold War successors, even extending to the current trend of emphasising conventional counter-proliferation in public pronouncements while incorporating such missions in operational nuclear policy.

It was also during the Kennedy administration that concern also grew about the strategic implications of China's potential nuclear capability, which was increasingly revealed by US surveillance of China in the early 1960s. It was the US view that 'the position of the Soviet leadership on peaceful coexistence and the dangers of nuclear escalation was substantially more responsible and less dangerous than Beijing's'.[31] Serious discussions on unilateral or joint US–Soviet preventive action against Chinese nuclear facilities were initiated and China even became the primary justification for the *Sentinel* anti-ballistic missile (ABM) system. To be sure, the Johnson administration rejected preventive action against China and instead undertook a massive intelligence campaign and initial ABM deployments.

However, the Chinese episode remains the only instance during the Cold War where this type of proliferation problem was considered a truly 'strategic' challenge, albeit briefly.

The post-MAD period: towards a 'prevailing' strategy

Mutual deterrence was based on the idea of assured-destruction parity between the US and the Soviet Union. While both countries arguably maintained an assured second-strike capability, under Nikita Khrushchev the Soviets still lagged far behind the US forces in terms of the number of strategic weapons and delivery systems. This changed with Leonid Brezhnev's rise to power. Between 1965 and 1966, new missile sites appeared throughout the Soviet Union. By the 1970s, the Soviet Union had reached numerical parity with its ICBMs and was exerting considerable energy to reach parity in SLBMs. The advent of multiple independently targetable re-entry vehicle (MIRV) technology further complicated the issue. Previously, one rocket booster would carry one re-entry vehicle (RV) warhead. With MIRV technology, one rocket booster could launch a 'bus' carrying numerous RVs that could be detached and launched at different targets. The fact that the Soviets were developing large rockets, which would eventually be able to carry more MIRVs than the *Minuteman* equivalent, created the possibility of a Soviet counter-force advantage against the American ICBM force.

Neither the Kennedy nor Johnson administrations were overly alarmed by the Soviet build-up, largely due to the prevalent perception that once the Soviets had developed an assured-destruction capability against the US, further nuclear capabilities would no longer be strategically significant. But the Nixon administration, by way of contrast, approached the actual attainment of nuclear parity and the potential problems that such a situation posed with trepidation. As Admiral Thomas Moorer, chairman of the JCS in 1970, noted: 'We do think today, now that we have this situation of approximate parity, that a mutual deterrent exists.'[32] The political ramifications of parity and mutual deterrence were certainly significant. This was a period during which America's confidence and security guarantees were being questioned owing to the debacle of Vietnam. The advent of MAD was seen as increasing the importance of the psychological balance, insofar as one side would need to convince an adversary – by obtaining more lethal capabilities or by signalling irrational 'madman' decision-making – that a nuclear threat was credible. Perceived American weakness was seen as seriously aggravating this issue.

One should not, however, underestimate the military threat posed by strategic parity. Nuclear parity between the two superpowers was seen as bringing the credibility of American extended deterrence guarantees in Western Europe into question. Given the Soviet capability for assured destruction of the United States, the promise of the American deployment of nuclear weapons in defence of Europe – which was seen as being suicidal given any attendant Soviet nuclear retaliation – sounded hollow indeed. The rapid nature of the Soviet build-up also raised questions as to whether the Soviets would be satisfied with parity or seek superiority. By mid-1975, the Soviet Union had not only reached parity with the US nuclear forces but, in terms of land-based forces, had exceeded them. Fourth-generation ICBMs with greatly improved accuracy and substantial throw-weights, the SS-17, SS-18 and SS-19, were being deployed. While all three were larger than their American equivalent, the SS-18 was particularly worrisome; in contrast to the *Minuteman* III's three MIRVs, it was able to carry eight. In addition, the Soviet navy was busy improving its SLBM forces, specifically with two improved ballistic missiles with ranges of 8,000 km (one of which was 'MIRVed') and the construction of the new *Typhoon*-class ballistic-missile submarine (SSBN). The Soviet *Backfire* bomber was reportedly improved with aerial refuelling technology and cruise missile weapons, numerous ICBM silos were 'superhardened' and construction of an extensive civil-defence system – including ABM deployments around Moscow – continued apace.[33] In response to these developments, US administrations from Richard Nixon to Reagan pursued three inter-related developments which would altogether modify American nuclear doctrine, expand on its existing targeting policy and set the foundations for the most recent evolutionary phase of US nuclear strategy.

Nuclear doctrine

While MAD would never be fully rejected by any subsequent administration, numerous modifications to the doctrine would be made. Under the Nixon administration, the achievement of a 'balance of terror' with the Soviet Union and the possibility of a Soviet 'assured destruction edge' led the United States to announce the idea of 'sufficiency'. This refers to the need to maintain forces that are able to inflict a sufficient level of damage against an aggressor in order to deter him, which would in turn ensure that America's ability and resolve to protect its interests were not underestimated. Four specific criteria were highlighted: a secure second-strike capability; avoidance of provocative measures; assurance that US damage and destruction did not exceed that of the Soviet Union in any attack; and deployment of defences to limit the damage of small or accidental attacks.[34] To help secure this capability, Secretary of Defense

Melvin Laird introduced the doctrine of the nuclear triad, which effectively rationalised and justified the pre-existing policy on the strategic nuclear arsenal. This doctrine called for each leg of the triad of ICBMs, SLBMs and bombers to maintain an independent second-strike deterrent capability, which would better allow the United States to negate any possible Soviet first strike.[35]

The Nixon administration was also aghast at the massively destructive nature of the nuclear-use options in American war plans. The long-standing desire for 'flexible' nuclear plans may have created five different attack options (both pre-emptive and retaliatory), but each one still consisted of a massive overkill strike against Soviet targets. As National Security Advisor Henry Kissinger later remarked on this 'horror strategy', 'to have the only option that of killing 80 million people is the height of immorality'.[36] In response, Kissinger would seek to include more 'limited nuclear attacks' in the range of targeting options in order to reinforce and make more credible the extended deterrence of Europe, and indeed to forestall Soviet belligerence in other regions. Despite his track record of winning bureaucratic battles, Kissinger faced considerable hostility for such planning from the Pentagon and had little success in these initial efforts.

American defence planners would, however, soon undergo a change of heart. By 1974, Secretary of Defense James Schlesinger, who had maintained deep scepticism of the entire MAD concept and often advocated an alternative war-fighting role, would announce what later became known as the 'Schlesinger Doctrine'. In an attempt to escape the credibility problem of MAD, this doctrine focused on having 'targeting options which are more selective and which do not necessarily involve major mass destruction on the other side'.[37] In an age of nuclear parity, such measures were seen as increasing the credibility of American nuclear threats and decreasing the possibility that the United States would be 'self-deterred' from threatening to use these weapons in response to Soviet belligerence. This was meant to provide the United States with 'escalation control', which signified the potential to undertake a limited attack and, owing to various 'withhold' options that would hold important enemy interests (e.g. population, socio-economic targets) hostage, prevent an adversary from escalating to a higher level of violence. In other words, the focus on escalation control is indicative of the post-MAD attempt to prevent the Soviet Union from dominating the escalation process and obtaining any political advantages from such dominance. This movement towards an 'assured destruction edge', while reinforcing the precepts of deterrence (especially extended deterrence), also contained hints of the need to plan for a winnable nuclear war if deterrence indeed failed.[38] The doctrine would be enshrined under National Security Decision Memorandum 242 (NSDM-242).

This focus on escalation control became increasingly important as the Soviet build-up of 'MIRVed' missiles with substantial throw-weights continued. According to the 'Nitze Scenario', the growing Soviet advantage in counter-force and hard-target-kill capabilities meant that it could conceivably destroy the majority of the American ICBM force and still have sufficient capabilities to deter any retaliation by threatening the destruction of US counter-value targets. The Soviet Union would thereby obtain an advantage in the ratio of residual forces after a nuclear exchange.[39] In response, the Carter administration outlined what Secretary of Defense Harold Brown on August 1980 labelled the 'countervailing strategy'. This re-evaluation of targeting policy and goals was the result of an 18-month study under the Nuclear Targeting Policy Review, which resulted in the codification of the countervailing strategy under Presidential Directive 59 on *Nuclear Weapons Employment Policy*. According to this nuclear doctrine, the United States would maintain 'countervailing strategic options such that at a variety of levels of exchange, aggression would either be defeated or would result in unacceptable costs that exceed gains'.[40] The ability to match the Soviet Union's capabilities, at various conflict levels, would thereby help ensure that the Soviets were indeed *fully* deterred from undertaking aggression.

The Reagan administration never used the term 'countervailing', but it appears to have followed its predecessor remarkably closely and, in fact, expanded on the precepts of this strategy to its natural conclusion. The Carter administration sought limited options to match the Soviets and thereby to hamper their ability to dominate the escalation process. Yet it remained more ambiguous on the implicit 'dominance' that any such control seemed to imply. A 'countervailing' strategy was based on the 'need to deny the Soviet Union a range of limited nuclear options rather than to develop these options for the United States'.[41] The Reagan administration was more explicit in its desire to achieve 'escalation dominance' that could 'contain or defeat the adversary at all levels of violence with the possible exception of the highest'.[42] War-fighting capabilities would, therefore, be needed in order to reinforce general deterrence, to give the US a measure of intrawar deterrence during conflict and, if necessary, to allow for satisfactory war termination in the event of full nuclear war. It seems fair to say that 'countervailing' had indeed been replaced with a 'prevailing' strategy, insofar as the National Security Decision Directive of October 1981 had the goal of prevailing in a protracted nuclear war of up to 180 days.[43]

Nuclear-targeting policy

American nuclear-weapons targeting policy continued and even expanded on what has always been a de facto counter-value *and* counter-force policy.[44] The Nixon administration followed McNamara's early emphasis on no-cities targeting by seeking more limited and discriminate nuclear options. This was designed to achieve both flexibility and selectivity. Flexibility referred to having numerous pre-planned target sets and retargeting capability, while selectivity was based on the actual grouping of targets and the need to minimise collateral damage.[45] Following NSDM-242, this targeting policy was initially enshrined under the Nuclear Weapons Employment Policy (NUWEP) guidance of 4 April 1974 and later formed the foundation of SIOP-5 on 1 January 1976. This provided a number of different nuclear options (including selective, regional and limited) and enshrined the Soviet recovery economy as a central 'withhold' option. The inclusion of the recovery economy had the effect of increasing the number of DGZs in urban-industrial areas in the Soviet Union, with an attendant increase in counter-value destruction in the event of a prolonged nuclear exchange.

The focus on finding targets that the Soviet leaders valued would be further refined under the Carter administration. After undergoing a major Nuclear Targeting Policy Review between 1977–79 and the issuing of NUWEP-80 in October 1980, the targeting policy moved towards political rather than economic recovery, and included 'the leadership and cadres of the Communist Party, KGB headquarters, Soviet internal security forces, and perhaps the army units along the Chinese borders' alongside some advocacy for the 'ethnic targeting' of the Russian population.[46] Emphasis on more survivable command, control and communications (C^3) was also incorporated in order to reduce the threat of 'decapitation' and to support intrawar deterrence and protracted nuclear warfare.[47]

With the issue of NUWEP-82 by the Reagan administration, which guided the creation of the SIOP-6 plan, the counter-economic recovery mission was replaced with a narrower emphasis on war-supporting industries. Hard-target-kill weapons were prioritised, including: missile-experimental (MX) ICBMs that could carry 10 MIRVs, *Trident* II D-5 SLBMs that combined high-yield 'MIRVed' warheads with greatly improved accuracy; nuclear air-launched cruise missiles (ALCMs) on the B-52 and B-1B aircraft, alongside the development of the B-2 stealth bomber; and the land-attack *Tomahawk* sea-launched cruise missiles.[48] These counter-force weapons were specifically directed at Soviet mobile weapons, leadership and C^3 systems. Guidance was provided by the release of annual NUWEPs and the formulation of six revisions to the SIOP nuclear-war plan (SIOP-6A to SIOP-6F). While an attack on the Soviet leadership was considered a withhold option for most of the 1980s, this policy changed on October 1989 with the advent of SIOP-6F, which called for prompt counter-leadership and counter-C^3 capabilities. According to Scott Sagan and Robert Toth, 'the new plan represent[ed] the most radical change in both the substance and structure of the US strategic nuclear war plan since the preparation of SIOP-63 in 1961–62'.[49]

Strategic missile defence

The growing emphasis on escalation control and dominance led to a growing interest in ABM systems capable of reducing the vulnerability of US society to a nuclear attack and assuring the survivability of the American strategic forces and C^3 systems. The US interest in missile-defence systems reflected a long-standing desire to obtain active defences against nuclear-delivery systems. In the 1950s and early 1960s, the United States initiated a number of air-defence measures to intercept Soviet nuclear-armed bombers, including the deployment of nuclear-armed interceptor squadrons and SAM batteries, a network of early-warning radars in Northern Canada and the Arctic, and the creation of the North American Air Defence Command to better coordinate continental air defence.[50] The advent of the ballistic missile changed this strategic calculus, as it increased the importance of the early-warning detection of any ICBM launch and refocused American interest in active defences to protect against incoming ballistic missiles.

The Johnson administration considered the possibility of a *Sentinel* ABM system that would protect the United States against a nuclear-armed China and, on a more implicit level, the Soviet Union. As pointed out by D.G. Brennan: 'much of the support (both inside and outside the Government) for the Sentinel decision came from those who believed that the system would eventually have significant capability against large Soviet attacks'.[51] In response to the growing threat posed by the Soviet 'MIRVed' ICBM forces, the Nixon administration authorised the deployment of the *Safeguard* ABM system, which was meant to provide limited protection to the US *Minuteman* ICBMs and command-and-control systems. However, both Johnson and Nixon pursued an agreement to ban the deployments of ABMs, which eventually resulted in the 1972 ABM Treaty, which only allowed for a limited deployment of ABM systems to the country's capital and an area containing ICBM silo launchers.

While the deployment of missile defences was restrained by the ABM Treaty, research and development on the military feasibility of ABM technology continued throughout the 1970s and 1980s. This culminated in the Reagan administration's particular vision of strategic relations between the two superpowers, which the president announced on 23 March 1983. Rather than relying on nuclear weapons as deterrents, Reagan offered a vision where 'we could intercept and destroy strategic ballistic missiles before they reached our soil or that of our allies'. In 1984, the Department of Defense (DoD) submitted to Congress a Strategic Defense Initiative (SDI), which was 'a long-term research and development program' to provide missile-defence options for subsequent administrations. The Reagan administration's vision for the SDI was nothing if not ambitious – the 'ultimate goal of eliminating the threat posed by strategic nuclear missiles' would have made nuclear weapons 'impotent and obsolete'.[52] The American population would be protected against a Soviet nuclear attack. An extensive range of interceptor options was considered, with a particular emphasis on space-based directed-energy weapons and battle stations armed with kinetic-energy interceptors.[53]

This represented an extreme vision for the SDI, dubbed 'Star Wars' by its critics. The requirement for population defence was, however, later de-emphasised by the administration. It would be replaced with the more feasible protection of vulnerable US ICBMs, and command-and-control facilities. US ICBM survivability would be increased, while the threat of decapitation would recede. However, there were important 'implications of shifting from a national strategy based on offensive deterrence to one based on both offensive and defensive weapon systems'.[54] A natural linkage exists between a counter-force capability and missile defence, as Reagan acknowledged: 'If paired with offensive systems [strategic defences] can be viewed as fostering an aggressive policy'.[55] As noted earlier, his administration initiated highly ambitious nuclear counter-force policies, including the development of hard-target-kill weapons and a fixation on disarming strikes, and counter-C^3 and counter-leadership targeting. Even a limited SDI, combined with these counter-force capabilities, promised a US ability to dominate escalation and, as feared by the Soviets, the potential for a US first-strike capability.[56] The SDI may have led the Soviet Union to expend scarce resources on its strategic offensive and defensive capabilities and contributed to the economic collapse of the Soviet adversary (though to what degree is debatable). This beneficial outcome must be balanced by the destabilising strategic dynamic that took place during the 'Second Cold War', which was only mitigated by the administration's rediscovery of arms control in its second term.

CHAPTER TWO

The Rise of American Counter-proliferation Policy

During the Cold War, American nuclear strategy was explicitly directed at deterring the threat posed by the Soviet Union's substantial conventional and, later, nuclear capabilities. The critical questions were always about the appropriate means of dealing with this threat, whether this meant the early flirtation with preventive-war-planning, the need for unilateral deterrence based on nuclear superiority or, in the Cold War's latest phase, the war-fighting deterrence by denial capabilities that were manifest during the Reagan administration. With the collapse of the Soviet Union, the threat perception that had comfortably guided the containment strategy of the United States for over 40 years diminished. It is true that the military capabilities designed with the Soviet Union in mind would be equally adequate for various other lesser security contingencies, as was clearly shown in the 1990–91 Gulf War, but as Secretary of Defense Les Aspin later acknowledged, 'It would be really impossible to overstate the degree to which our defense planning focused on the Soviet Union ... It determined the size of the defense budget, the kinds of divisions we had, how we organized our forces ... even how we designed weapons.'[1]

In contrast, the strategic threat environment after the Cold War was more diverse and uncertain. A whole range of possible threat scenarios was recognised as posing potentially serious short- and/or long-term challenges. Yet a new consensus gradually formed on the strategic dangers posed by the horizontal proliferation of WMD to such regional adversaries as North Korea, Iran and, prior to its 2003 invasion, Iraq. As Gilles Andreani points out, while the Pentagon went through numerous scenarios ranging from peacekeeping to large-scale regional conflicts, 'only those involving nuclear, biological and chemical weapons ... could conceivably pose a direct threat to the United States and its population'.[2] Neither the 'global war on terror', nor the 'counter-proliferation war' into Iraq, with its flawed WMD justifications and its subsequent messy incarnation as a counter-insurgency campaign, appear to have seriously damaged this consensus.

The new triad strategy clearly reinforced the important role that WMD-armed rogue states play in the American nuclear posture. A proactive counter-proliferation policy strategy to deal with the 'post-proliferated and terror-prone security environment' has since become a key pillar of the wider US national security strategy.[3] The National Security Presidential Directive 17 (NSPD-17) on *National Strategy to Combat Weapons of Mass Destruction*, which offered further presidential legitimisation of the Pentagon's efforts to develop unilateral counter-proliferation measures, reflects this.[4] It would, however, be a mistake to consider this revision of American nuclear strategy a fundamental change. Since the dissolution of the Soviet Union, the United States has increasingly perceived regional adversaries as the most significant strategic threats. This has led to changes not only to conventional military doctrine, but also to nuclear doctrine and operational policy that, in turn, have played an integral role in the formation of the Bush administration's own nuclear strategy. The evolution of American nuclear strategy did not end with the demise of the Soviets, but was simply reformulated – albeit with a different rationale – to deal with new adversaries in a more complex threat environment.

Origins of the 'rogue-state doctrine'

The American perception of regional adversaries as 'rogues' or 'outlaws' has clear parallels with the Cold War. As Richard Betts notes, 'Many today forget that Stalin's Soviet Union and Mao Zedong's China were seen as more threatening in both capabilities and intentions than are today's mullahs in Tehran'[5] or, for that matter, the paranoid rulers in Pyongyang. According to NSC-68, the United States confronted a Soviet Union that was ruled by a 'despotic oligarchy', imbued with a 'fanatic new faith' and fixated on 'world domination'. The resultant Cold War, especially in its early years, represented a dangerous 'zero-sum game' in which 'confrontation was the order of the day, and ideology justified the confrontational nature of the relationship'.[6] It should, therefore, come as no surprise that an influential 1994 article by Anthony Lake, Assistant to the President for National Security Affairs during the administration of Bill Clinton, would invoke George Kennan's strategy against the Soviet 'outlaw empire' in defence of the rogue-state doctrine and the attendant dual containment of Iraq and Iran.[7]

This alarmist threat perception echoes that of the early 1960s, when the Chinese regime under Mao came closer to acquiring a nuclear capability. Indeed, this regime shared many characteristics attributed to rogue states, including extreme belligerence, support for insurgencies and terrorist organisations, a fixation on WMD and a potentially undeterrable leadership. This led not only to the serious consideration of preventive war, but also to the formation of the high-level Gilpatric Committee, under former Undersecretary of Defense Roswell Gilpatric, to discuss possible responses to the dangers of nuclear proliferation.[8] The committee recommended a more aggressive approach to the proliferation problem that, while quietly rejected by the Johnson administration, would serve as an important foundation for the development of the non-proliferation regime. The Non-Proliferation Treaty (NPT), which forms the bedrock of this regime, would be signed some years later in 1968.

China's acquisition of nuclear weapons also raised the spectre of the '*N*th country problem', whereby an unknown number of countries, having sufficient technical capabilities, would eventually build nuclear weapons. The '*N*th country experiment' that took place at Lawrence Radiation Laboratory in the mid-1960s, where two young physicists created a workable implosion-fission-bomb design from unclassified data, demonstrated the technical feasibility of this danger.[9] However, this issue would soon decline in importance. The much-anticipated '*N*th country' was found to be Israel, which acquired a nuclear arsenal in the 1960s and 1970s. Yet Israel did not emerge as an open nuclear power and its undeclared status would, after some deliberation, even be secretly accepted by the Nixon administration.[10] Nor did the Chinese example spur an immediate cascade of proliferation as it was originally feared, in that Japan would continue to rely on American security guarantees, and nuclear events in South Asia would remain opaque and ambiguous until the nuclear tests of 1997. Indeed, the dangers associated with the *N*th country, and the attendant proliferation that was implicit in the concept, would not *immediately* arise.[11]

American concerns over proliferation during the Cold War were largely focused on a number of its allies that, owing to their precarious security environments, were tempted by the nuclear option. These states included Israel, South Africa, Taiwan and South Korea. These nuclear proliferators would eventually be cajoled with a mixture of carrots and sticks to stay non-nuclear, or in certain cases (namely Israel and South Africa) to remain undeclared nuclear powers. These examples, however, suggested a more troubling scenario: that of an aggressive regional military power that could challenge American security interests. An assortment of countries were considered potential threats, including Egypt, India, North Korea, Iraq, Iran and Syria. Concerns over 'regional powers' led to the Presidential Commission on Integrated Long-Term Strategy January 1988 report, entitled *Discriminate Deterrence*, which clearly noted the potential threat posed by emerging regional states, their 'sizable arms industries' and military capabilities. As the report goes on to note, 'The [expanding] arsenals of the lesser powers will make it riskier and more difficult for the superpowers to intervene in regional wars.'[12]

The role of regional powers in US military strategy was also gradually expanding. During the Cold War, while the United States was often involved in regional scenarios, any regional approach was grounded in and dependent upon the broader Cold War context. A primary example was the formulation of the 'Carter Doctrine', which had a regional focus but was largely concerned with an external threat: 'Any attempt by any outside force to gain control of the Persian Gulf region will be regarded as an assault on the vital interests of the United States of America'.[13] Yet it also contained the seeds of a more independently regional approach, insofar as it raised the possibility that a state could, with sufficient military capabilities, also seize control of its own vital strategic region.[14] Attention would continue to be paid to the external threat during the 1980s, but the 'Reagan Corollary' to the Carter Doctrine, which noted that the United States would not allow a hostile force to take over Saudi Arabia and cut off its oil supply, can be seen as a subtle warning against ambitious external *and* internal powers. An explicit regional defence policy would be fully articulated in the George H.W. Bush administration's 'New Defense Strategy' of 1990, and would be codified in the January 1993 *Regional Defense Strategy* and its call for a 'base force' that would be capable of fighting in two major regional conflicts (MRCs).[15]

Further modifications to this new 'regional' concern would soon be evident. The United States became fixated on certain regional states that were repressive, undertook destabilising external behaviour and, perhaps most importantly, were adversarial to the United States (and vice versa). As noted by Robert Litwak, the origins of the term 'rogue state' can be traced to the State Department's list of state sponsors of terrorism and the combination of 'internal' and 'external' characteristics that marked these 'outlaw states'.[16] The military capabilities of a regional power were important, as they represented its *capability* to pose a threat to the United States, but the growing emphasis on the political nature of the state's regime and the threatening character of its external policies marked a turn towards incorporating *intention* as an indicator of whether a regional power indeed represented a 'threat'. The contemporary emphasis on 'rogue states' was slowly being moulded.

Sponsorship of terrorism would remain an important component of the 'external behaviour' that would mark rogue states. But it would be joined by American concern over an adversary's unconventional weapon capabilities, including CB weapons, as a key variable in the seriousness of this new strategic threat. In December 1988, Central Intelligence Agency Director William H. Webster spoke at length on the dangers posed by the proliferation of WMD and ballistic-missile delivery systems, and only a year later Secretary of State James Baker would speak at his confirmation hearing on the threat of chemical weapons in the hands of governments prone to aggression and terrorism. These comments were reinforced by a series of Congressional committee hearings on the dangers of horizontal proliferation towards the end of the 1980s, and the growing interest of Pentagon officials in the need to operate in a WMD-environment.[17] Nuclear weapons would remain the most devastating and, therefore, troubling of these unconventional threats, owing to their arguably unparalleled destructive capability, but proliferation concerns were no longer limited to nuclear arms.

American threat perception in the post-Cold War period would be dominated by a 'characterization of hostile (or seemingly hostile) Third World States with large military forces and nascent WMD capabilities as "rogue states" or "nuclear outlaws" bent on sabotaging the prevailing world order'.[18] The shift from a global to a regional approach, which was one of the results of the demise of the global Soviet 'peer competitor' that challenged (and perhaps rationalised) the dominant American strategic position, led naturally to a renewed focus on these revisionist adversaries – the so-called 'rogue states' – that had the potential capability and interest to challenge the United States in their respective regions.

This 'rogue-state doctrine' was not simply about the direct asymmetrical threat that these regional adversaries posed to American interests. Given the potential that a rogue state armed with WMD could trigger a regional proliferation cascade, this doctrine was also implicitly linked to the post-Cold War American drive to maintain and expand its global strategic primacy. A cascade of WMD proliferation, most acutely with nuclear weapons, could have lead to a strong incentive for prominent non-nuclear countries, such as Germany and Japan, to 'go nuclear', and indeed could have sparked vertical nuclear-weapon build-ups by established powers. This would have represented a relative decline in American primacy and, thereby, facilitated the rise of a future near-peer competitor. This connection is highlighted in the draft Defense Planning Guidance (DPG) of 1992, which according to Patrick Tyler argued that:

> Nuclear proliferation, if unchecked by superpower action, could tempt Germany, Japan and other industrial powers to acquire nuclear weapons to deter attack from regional foes. This could start them down the road to global competition with the United States and, in a crisis over national interests, military rivalry.[19]

The DPG was, after it was leaked to the media, redrafted in a more diplomatic and multilateral tone. Yet the final document, which avoids talk of actively preventing the rise of a peer competitor, would still maintain a strong 'primacist' inclination – the United States would concentrate on 'shaping the future security environment', and thereby assuring that its strategic primacy would be sufficient to dissuade competition.[20] The rogue-state doctrine would play an important role in these efforts to shape the future security environment.

The counter-proliferation initiative

During the Cold War, the United States relied primarily on a number of bilateral and multilateral non-proliferation measures to deal with WMD proliferation, aimed largely (but not exclusively) at regulating the supply of weapons and their related technology to states.[21] Various non-proliferation measures continued into the 1990s and achieved some remarkable results. South Africa eliminated its small nuclear arsenal, while Belarus, Kazakhstan and Ukraine transferred the Soviet nuclear weapons on their territory to Russia. The proliferation dangers posed by the significant Russian arsenal and expertise in WMD were mitigated, if not eliminated, by US–Russian Cooperative Threat Reduction activities initiated in the early 1990s. Meanwhile, Latin America finally became a nuclear-weapons-free zone when Brazil and Argentina gave up their nuclear-weapons ambitions and signed both the Treaty of Tlatelolco and the NPT. Perhaps the high point of this non-proliferation movement was at the 1995 NPT Review Conference, when the US convinced the non-nuclear states to extend the NPT indefinitely.[22]

However, despite these successes, the perception arose that horizontal WMD proliferation to rogue states posed an increasingly important strategic challenge. Indeed, the realisation that the US might have to undertake combat operations in a WMD environment clearly arose in the case of Iraq, the prototypical rogue state. The 1990–91 Gulf War featured the implicit threat of CB use by Saddam Hussein's regime, a possibility that was made all the more credible due to the extensive use of chemical weapons during the preceding Iran–Iraq War. This led the United States to undertake not only active and passive defences for its troops, but also to attempt conventional strikes to pre-empt possible the use of unconventional weapons by Iraq.[23] In 1994, Lieutenant-General Hussein Kamel, head of Iraq's unconventional weapons programmes, revealed an Iraqi biological-weapons capability that was far more advanced than had been anticipated.[24] The fact that Iraq had aerial bombs and missiles filled with aflatoxin, anthrax and botulinum toxin deployed at four sites during the Gulf War revealed how close American forces had come to potentially dealing with 'germ warfare'.[25]

The Clinton administration eventually embraced its predecessor's regional two-MRC military strategy, evident in the 1993 release of the Bottom-Up Review (BUR), and quickly followed it with the public articulation of the DoD's new counter-proliferation mission. A Defense Counterproliferation Initiative (DCI), which was seen as being a critical adjunct to the traditional non-proliferation regime, was unveiled in Aspin's speech to the National Academy of Sciences on 7 December 1993 and would be codified under Presidential Decision Directive 18 (PDD-18). In the event of WMD proliferation taking place, in spite of the best efforts of the non-proliferation regime, the DCI would ensure that the United States would still be able to provide a degree of protection against this threat, either through passive and active defences or by destroying WMD capabilities with pre-emptive counter-force strikes. 'At the heart of the Defense Counterproliferation Initiative, therefore, is a drive to develop new military capabilities to deal with this new threat'.[26]

A key component of this new DoD mission was the preparation for combating WMD in future battlefields, through changes in defence-planning guidance, contingency planning, doctrine, equipment, training and intelligence coordination. The new position of assistant secretary of defense for nuclear security and counterproliferation was created, and the development and acquisition of counter-proliferation capabilities was accelerated under the Counterproliferation Support Program (and overseen by the high-level Counterproliferation Program Review Committee). A Counterproliferation Council was formed as a coordinating body in the DoD, and a Counterproliferation Concept Plan (CONPLAN 0400) was developed for the planning of national-level counter-proliferation policy in terms of objectives and supporting tasks, which was used by the regional commanders to develop their own area-specific counter-proliferation CONPLANs. According to Barry Schneider, the DCI introduced a new mission that 'require[d] improved active and passive defenses, development of large area decontamination capabilities after suffering NBC [nuclear, biological and chemical] attacks, improved deterrence against regional adversaries armed with small but growing NBC arsenals, and improved counterforce capabilities to destroy adversary WMD should that prove absolutely necessary'.[27]

The logic of the two-MRC strategy, and the need for appropriate counter-proliferation tools during any such theatre engagement, was reinforced in the 1994 North Korean nuclear crisis. Military options were severely limited during this crisis and American defence planners were well aware of the potentially catastrophic consequences of such an MRC – it was estimated that the US and South Korean military would suffer 300,000 to 500,000 casualties in the first 90 days, with civilian casualties numbering in the hundreds of thousands.[28] Massive amounts of conventional artillery deployed near the de-militarised zone were a significant concern, yet scenarios also involved North Korea's suspected CB-weapons capability and the potential problems that American troops would have fighting in a WMD environment. Pyongyang's offensive-strike capability against such regional allies as Japan, with their crucially important forward-deployed bases, were considered a particular danger – the North has an extensive ballistic-missile programme and such missiles could have been mated with either CB agents or, in the worst-case scenario, a small nuclear device. Reports even indicate that the United States, cognisant of these dangers yet also aware of how destabilising a nuclear-armed North Korea might have been, briefly considered pre-emptive military action during the nuclear crisis.[29]

Defensive capabilities are central to American counter-proliferation efforts. Passive measures are meant to mitigate the impact of a WMD (and especially CB) attack – this can be done by implementing protective measures for units, personnel and civilians from the hazards of CB agents, as well as through the decontamination of a WMD-contaminated environment. Active defences play a complementary role in the reduction of missiles, aircraft and other delivery systems from successfully delivering WMD to their targets. This lessens the degree of WMD-contamination and passive-defence requirements at key sites, and would be the only feasible way to defend against the most destructive (e.g. nuclear) WMD. The importance of active defences like BMD is clearly reiterated in CONPLAN 0400, which is the long-standing (and continuously updated) campaign plan for US counter-proliferation efforts.[30] In effect, the US would be able to undertake counter-proliferation missions against WMD-armed rogue states more freely, while reducing the probability of successful retaliation by those adversaries.

BMD would continue to be developed in the post-Cold War period. Yet the rationale for such defences would be firmly rooted in the need to eliminate the relatively limited and often short-range capabilities of rogue-state proliferators. This trend began under the Bush Snr administration, which transformed the SDI into the more limited Global Protection Against Limited Strikes (GPALS). GPALS would be designed to use the 'Brilliant Pebbles' kinetic-energy system from the SDI programme to intercept a limited attack by a regional adversary, or in the case of an accidental Soviet missile attack. This was followed by the Clinton administration's prioritisation of theatre missile-defence (TMD) programmes, alongside tactical point-defence systems, as opposed to any multi-tiered national missile defence (NMD) capable of a 'thick defence' of the continental United States. This was partly due to the salience of this issue, insofar as many rogue states had already developed short- and medium-range missiles that were capable of holding at risk American forward-deployed forces, their regional bases and their allies. Active defences designed to protect a relatively smaller area from ballistic-missile strikes were also considered a more feasible option that, unlike a NMD system, would not be considered a challenge to strategic nuclear stability.

A TMD system uses a 'kill vehicle' to intercept and destroy an incoming missile through kinetic (hit-to-kill) energy. It would, however, be a less ambitious system capable of protecting a limited area; the two most common scenarios associated with the two-MRC military strategy were the protection of American troops and allies in the Middle East and Northeast Asia regions. Tactical missile defences, a subset of TMD, are designed to protect the US military forces and basing areas against the battlefield use of WMD. Both programmes are heavily interconnected, insofar as a tactical system could be deployed in sufficient numbers to provide a theatre-level capability. Theatre and tactical missile-defence programmes proliferated under the Clinton administration in the 1990s. For example, the US began deploying the *Patriot* Advanced Capability 3 (PAC-3) tactical system and would actively research a number of different boost-, midcourse- and terminal-phase TMD systems, including the Airborne Laser (ABL), the Theater High Altitude Area Defense (THAAD) system, the Navy Area Wide system and the Navy Theater Wide (NTW) system. In addition, the United States pursued joint TMD programmes with numerous allies, including the *Arrow* system with Israel and the Medium Extended Air Defense System (MEADS) with Germany and Italy.

The Clinton administration did, however, oversee the gradual if reluctant move towards a NMD system that would be capable of protecting the US from a small number of ballistic missiles; the central scenarios were a limited attack from a rogue state and an accidental or unauthorised strike by an established nuclear power. The Clinton administration was initially quite circumspect in its support for strategic missile defence and questioned its technological readiness. In the 1993 BUR, TMD programmes were allocated $12 billion over the course of five years, in contrast to the $3bn allocated for NMD.[31] Yet pressure for an unambiguous national missile-defence policy was increasing. Perhaps the most high-profile rationale was provided by the July 1998 release of the *Report of the Commission to Assess the Ballistic Missile Threat to the United States*, which stated that North Korea, Iran and Iraq 'would be able to inflict major destruction on the US within about five years of a decision to acquire such a capability (10 years in the case of Iraq)'.[32]

The growing calls by the Republican Party and especially its hawkish neo-conservative wing for a more robust policy against this 'imminent' intercontinental threat, alongside the Iranian testing of a *Shahab*-3 missile and the North Korean testing of a *Taepo-dong*-1 missile that seemed to vindicate the Commission's conclusions, eventually led to the signing of the 1999 National Missile Defense Act. Despite this grudging acceptance of the need for a continental 'area-defence' capability, funding for TMD systems still dominated the Clinton administration's approach to missile defence, with the FY2001 budget request called for $2.8bn for TMD in contrast to the $1.9bn for NMD.[33] Even the NMD vision consisted of a relatively limited deployment – the planned missile-defence architecture would have consisted of 250 interceptors at Alaska and North Dakota by 2011, and would only be hypothetically capable of protecting against several warheads. The failure of several interceptor flight tests, however, led Clinton to defer interceptor deployments for the subsequent administration.

'Nuclear counter-proliferation' in the 1990s

The DCI had a particular emphasis on the need for the United States to obtain conventional-strike capabilities to fight in a WMD environment. This new mission not only acknowledged the problems associated with the current non-proliferation regime, but also implicitly accepted that the US nuclear deterrent was insufficient to deter and retaliate against WMD-armed rogue states. This was made clear in the *Joint Doctrine for Operations in an NBC Environment*: 'Should deterrence fail, US forces will need to survive, avoid or mitigate the effects of NBC employment, fight, and win in a contaminated battlespace. Key to operational success may be the … ability to eliminate or reduce the adversary's capabilities with available and *appropriate means*.'[34]

However, it would be a mistake to assume that this trend towards counter-proliferation missions did not have an equally important impact on American nuclear strategy. The United States maintained a 'calculated ambiguity' nuclear doctrine against rogue states armed with CB weapons. While not specifying what response would be given in the event of a CB attack, the

US did state that any retaliatory response would be devastating. As pointed out by Secretary of Defense William Cohen in November 1998, 'We think the ambiguity involved in the issue of nuclear weapons contributes to our security, keeping any potential adversary who might use either chemical or biological [weapons] unsure of what our response would be.'[35] This doctrine was aptly demonstrated in the 1990–91 Gulf War, where senior US officials issued messages that nuclear weapons might be used in the event of an Iraqi CB attack. Perhaps the clearest warning came from a letter written by Bush Snr and delivered to Saddam Hussein on 5 January 1991, which warned that 'unconscionable acts' like the use of CB weapons would 'demand the strongest possible response' and that 'you and your country will pay a terrible price'.[36] It is true, however, that the credibility of these nuclear threats was far from robust. Not only did Iraq test these American 'red lines', for example by setting Kuwait's oil fields ablaze, but senior American leaders would even retrospectively dismiss the Bush Snr's nuclear threat.

Despite this doctrine of ambiguity, American nuclear-weapons targeting policy was openly focused on the threat posed by CB-armed rogue states throughout the 1990s. With the near-collapse of the Soviet Union, the JCS published a Military Net Assessment in March 1990 that cited 'increasingly capable Third World threats' as a new justification for maintaining nuclear weapons. This was a crucial endeavour, in that the end of the Cold War led to a substantial reduction of the nuclear-target list (from 10,000 to 2,500 entries[37]) and, therefore, a need to rationalise the existing nuclear-weapons infrastructure and arsenal. It is noteworthy that Secretary of Defense Dick Cheney's June 1990 testimony to the Senate Appropriations Committee focused on the horizontal proliferation of WMD as a key rationale for maintaining the US nuclear arsenal.[38]

The incorporation of counter-proliferation into American nuclear-targeting policy received a significant boost in the aftermath of the Gulf War. Immediately after Kuwait's liberation, the Bush Snr administration released a NUWEP that directed American nuclear-war planners to target regional CB capabilities. In March 1991, the Joint Military Net Assessment identified the utility of non-strategic weapons for these post-Cold War roles and recommended upgrades of American C^3 capabilities.[39] These developments led General Lee Butler, the commander of Strategic Command (STRATCOM), to establish a Deterrence Study Group chaired by former Secretary of the Air Force Thomas Reed and organised by the Joint Strategic Targeting Planning Staff. The Reed Panel, as it became known, began a process of threat monitoring that recommended an expansion of nuclear targeting against 'every reasonable adversary', even against non-nuclear-weapon states armed only with CB weapons.[40] While certain officials were alarmed with this notion, nuclear-war planning for contingences in the Third World continued unabated. The 1992 JSCP directed the retargeting of nuclear weapons towards Third World rogue states. The expansion of targets in the Third World would be formally codified on 1 June 1992 with SIOP-93. While the Bush Snr and Boris Yeltsin unilateral-disarmament initiatives complicated the process of new targeting options, an updated NUWEP-82 and JSCP were followed by a new deliberative nuclear-war plan in the spring of 1993 (SIOP-94) that reduced the number of targets but continued to emphasise the new targeting options. The need to deter all types of WMD and to use low-yield weapons for retaliation in the event of deterrence failure was also reiterated in the 1993 JCS's *Doctrine for Joint Nuclear Operations*.[41]

While the Clinton administration remained publicly ambiguous on the utility of nuclear weapons serving as a deterrent against CB capabilities, American nuclear-war planners were under no such illusion. The administration's disinterest in (or perhaps distaste for) this issue, alongside the complex and arcane nature of nuclear-war planning itself, led to STRATCOM's monopolisation of the planning process. At a time when the respective nuclear arsenals of both superpowers were undergoing a period of significant reductions in terms of tactical and intermediate-range weapon systems, STRATCOM would release a number of force-structure studies and briefings between 1991 and 1996 that put forward the command's view of what constituted a sufficient post-Cold War deterrent. The Phoenix Study of 1991 and the Sun City Study of 1993 advocated a reduced but still very robust force structure that effectively became codified in START II, while later studies – particularly Sun City Extended in 1994 – began to examine expanded-targeting requirements in China and rogue-state proliferators. The need to expand American nuclear counter-force capabilities, which would offer a war-fighting edge against any resurgent Russian threat and denial capabilities against strategic WMD assets among post-Cold War targets, were a constant theme throughout the studies.[42]

The expansion of American nuclear targets led to a renewed emphasis on more usable and low-yield nuclear warheads for counter-proliferation missions. Although plans for such weapons had been made during the 1980s, the end of serious East–West tension – and the need for new justifications and 'requirements' for the US nuclear arsenal – fostered a temporarily permissive environment to discuss their post-Cold War utility. Prominent scientists from US nuclear-weapon laboratories began advocating the development of tactical, war-fighting nuclear warheads (e.g. the 10-tonne 'micro-nukes', the 100-tonne 'mini-nuke' and the 1,000-tonne 'tiny-nuke') at a time when tactical nuclear weapons were being unilaterally reduced by both the United States and the Soviet Union.[43] The 1989 Nuclear Weapons Development Guidance advocated 'enhanced' and 'tailored' nuclear capabilities, while the Nuclear Weapons Council (NWC) endorsed low-yield earth-penetrating nuclear warheads. The USAF would even establish Project PLYWD (Precision Low-Yield Weapons Design), which was a research project to examine tactical-weapon concepts for use against Third World targets.[44] This advocacy would not go unchallenged, as a sceptical Congress in 1993 passed the Furse–Spratt amendment to the 1994 Defense Authorization Act that prevented research and development into the production of a low-yield (under 5-kilotonne) nuclear warhead.

It was in 1994 that the Clinton administration, during the lead-up to the NPR, belatedly attempted to rein in the hawkish nuclear policies that were being advocated and developed by the Pentagon and the nuclear-weapons laboratories. The six working groups of the 1994 NPR process were under the co-chair of Assistant Secretary of Defense Ashton Carter, who was seen as a proponent of significant nuclear-weapons reductions. Yet despite his best efforts, and those of Special Assistant Steven Fetter, the 1994 NPR effectively codified the earlier views of STRATCOM's force-structure studies. The counter-proliferation working group, despite misgivings by both Carter and Fetter, would also agree with STRATCOM on the 'unique' utility of nuclear weapons in counter-proliferation missions. This conclusion was minimised in the public record, yet 'when the results were briefed to Congress in September 1994, nuclear weapons featured prominently in counter-proliferation roles such as to "deter WMD acquisition or use"'.[45]

Buoyed by its success, STRATCOM attempted to further centralise American counter-proliferation efforts under its own command. This was purportedly to give the mission a global focus, while better matching WMD targets with actual US global military capabilities. To this end, STRATCOM initiated a project on the Strategic Installation List of Vulnerability Effects and Results, which is better known as the 'Silver Books project'. These were classified plans for counter-proliferation strikes against the WMD capabilities of rogue states.[46] A Silver Book was completed for European Command in 1994, while a prototype plan was being readied for Pacific Command. This project would be terminated in 1995, as STRATCOM's attempt at a greater role in counter-proliferation was challenged by regional commanders keen to assert their own authority on this issue. Yet STRATCOM would continue to incorporate counter-proliferation as an integral new mission for the US nuclear arsenal. The Strategic Advisory Group at STRATCOM released a 1995 review of its nuclear deterrence posture, entitled 'Essentials of Post-Cold

War Deterrence', that advocated not only a 'madman' approach to deterrence, but also the utility of using nuclear weapons to deter CB weapons.[47] Regional nuclear-war-planning scenarios were undertaken against Iran and North Korea, and this regional approach to nuclear-war-planning was codified in the JCS's 1996 *Doctrine for Joint Theater Nuclear Operations*. This would be followed a year later by the Clinton administration's still-classified PDD-60 on *Nuclear Weapons Employment Policy Guidance*, which may have overturned the Reagan administration's 1981 directive on 'prevailing' in a nuclear war, but also retroactively legitimised STRATCOM's efforts to expand nuclear-targeting options against China and rogue states.

Strategic force modernisation planned in the latter years of the Cold War as a means of dealing with more sophisticated Soviet capabilities would complement this vision by qualitatively enhancing American counter-force capabilities. The *Minuteman* III's 'Guidance Replacement Program' would improve the accuracy of the ICBM warhead, giving it a comparable CEP (circular error probable) to the MX hard-target-kill warhead and extend the service life of the weapon platform.[48] Meanwhile, even though the Furse–Spratt amendment may have limited the development of low-yield tactical weapons, the US would modify an existing nuclear warhead to obtain a modest earth-penetration capability (the B-61 Mod 11). This was developed with counter-proliferation missions in mind and was even brandished against Libya's suspected chemical-weapons facilities at Tarhunah in 1996.[49]

Rapid re-targeting capabilities were seen as crucial to 'adaptive' nuclear-war-plan generation, and equally useful against mobile ICBMs in established nuclear powers and for limited options against rogue states. The Navy's SLBM Retargeting System and the USAF's Rapid Execution and Combat Targeting system would give the American land- and sea-based strategic forces rapid re-targeting and target-processing capabilities. The modernisation of these systems was an integral part of STRATCOM's plan to develop a modernised, flexible, adaptive and global Strategic War Planning System (SWPS) to replace the archaic Cold-War-era guidance-planning system. The SWPS refers to the system used to formulate and develop American nuclear-war plans (to analyse and assign weapons to targets, and to deliver nuclear weapons).[50] The process of SWPS modernisation from 1993 to 2003 erased the traditional distinction between strategic and tactical nuclear planning, and the US enshrined 'adaptive planning' in a revolutionary 'Living SIOP' capable of creating a new plan in 4–6 months (rather than 14–18), undertaking limited options in 24 hours and re-targeting 1,000 targets per day.[51]

CHAPTER THREE

The Strategic Vision of the New Triad

The current Bush administration made its own mark on American nuclear strategy with the release of the 2002 NPR. This congressionally mandated review outlined a new triad based on offensive-strike systems (nuclear and non-nuclear), defences (active and passive) and a revitalised defence infrastructure to 'provide new capabilities in a timely fashion to meet emerging threats'.[1] An enhanced command, control and intelligence (C^2I) system would play a supporting role in binding the three legs of the new triad together.[2] This review was heavily informed by a 2001 study by the National Institute for Public Policy, entitled *Rationale and Requirements for US Nuclear Forces*, which advocated many of the same recommendations for its 'adaptable deterrence' posture. This included expanded targeting requirements, the incorporation of conventional offensive and defensive capabilities, and the need to prepare for deterrence failure.[3]

The NPR's strategic posture extends the shift from a 'threat-based' to a 'capabilities-based' model of defence planning, which, according to the 2001 *Quadrennial Defense Review* (QDR), emphasises 'how an adversary might fight [rather] than who the adversary might be or where a war might occur'.[4] The NPR recommends new nuclear-targeting options and notes the utility of developing 'credible', low-yield nuclear warheads. New nuclear capabilities are required to hold at risk a growing number of targets, particularly hardened and deeply buried targets (HDBTs) that can be used to protect WMD, C^3 systems and other strategic assets. Active defences could conceivably blunt a WMD 'bolt-out-of-the-blue' or retaliatory strike against US forces and allies abroad, as well as provide strategic defences against any spasm attack against North America.

The new triad's *mélange* of strategic capabilities is designed to deal with the 'diverse set of potential adversaries and unexpected threats the United States may confront in the coming decade'.[5] As the NPR goes on to note, 'North Korea, Iraq, Iran, Syria, and Libya are among the countries that could be involved in immediate, potential, or unexpected contingencies'.[6] This follows on from the Bush administration's heightened sense of alarm over WMD-armed rogue states that the events of 11 September 2001 accentuated. NSPD-17, for example, reiterated the American commitment to respond with 'overwhelming force, including potentially nuclear weapons', to a WMD attack by either a terrorist or a rogue state.[7] Indeed, as noted by Jason Ellis, the United States views the 'gravest danger' to be a threat nexus posed by the combination of rogue states, terrorists and WMD.[8] This perspective was forcefully made in the 2002 *National Security Strategy of the United States of America* (NSS): 'We must be prepared to stop rogue states and their terrorist clients before they are able to threaten or use weapons of mass destruction against the United States and our allies and friends.'[9]

The new-triad posture, if fully realised, is seen to enable the US to hold at risk an adversary's deterrent more effectively and, with its combination of usable nuclear weapons and missile defence, to threaten the use of its strategic capabilities more credibly. The strategy is still firmly rooted in the notions of *deterrence* against its adversaries and the *assurance* (e.g. extended deterrence guarantees) of its allies. These traditional notions have been complemented by more ambitious objectives. The *dissuasion* of potential adversaries from even pursuing threatening capabilities is now seen as a feasible possibility, while the *defeat* of an adversary in the event of deterrence failure has now been embraced.[10]

Offensive-strike systems

The 'offensive-strike' leg of the new triad incorporates the existing nuclear arsenal of ICBMs, SLBMs and nuclear-armed penetrating bombers, and integrates these traditional strategic nuclear-launch vehicles with new non-nuclear counter-force capabilities. The NPR also envisions a gradual qualitative 'transformation' of the American nuclear arsenal, which would be better tailored for counter-proliferation missions against rogue-state adversaries. New earth-penetrator weapons (EPWs) would be designed to be able to use sub-surface bursts and ground shock to destroy HDBTs, while agent-defeat weapons (ADWs) would, through various means, be able to neutralise or incinerate CB agents. Such specialised counter-force capabilities were seen as necessary to hold at risk for destruction an adversary's strategic military capabilities, and in the event of deterrence failure, to provide 'greater flexibility in the design and conduct of military campaigns to defeat opponents decisively'.[11]

The NPR envisions a force structure of 1,700–2,200 operationally deployed strategic warheads by 2012, which would consist of 14 *Trident* SSBNs, 500 *Minuteman* III ICBMs, 76 B-52H bombers and 21 B-2 bombers. Both Russia and the US agreed to this quantitative reduction in deployed warheads in the SORT. Implementation of the NPR/SORT reductions has already begun, with the current American operational nuclear warheads – as of early 2006 – reduced to an estimated 5,235 out of a total stockpile of nearly 10,000 active and inactive warheads. Since 2002, 50 MX missiles have been retired, though retained for possible future use, and four *Trident* II SSBNs have been removed from service and are being converted into conventional cruise-missile submarines.[12] According to the 2006 QDR, the planned force structure of the American land-based *Minuteman* III force will be further modified and reduced to 450 ICBMs.[13] In 2004, the Bush administration signed NSPD-34, a classified nuclear-weapons-stockpile plan for 2004 to 2012, and notified Congress that the total stockpile would be cut nearly in half.[14] This reduction promises to leave the United States with more than 3,000 warheads in storage for use as either active, non-deployed warheads in the 'responsive nuclear force' or as part of its 'inactive stockpile' of warheads that have critical components (e.g. tritium) removed.

Despite these reductions, ambitious modernisation plans for nuclear-legacy systems have continued apace. Indeed, strategic force modernisation promises to improve the already significant American ability to undertake counter-force missions against even established nuclear powers. An improvement in the accuracy of these high-yield warheads would, by being able to deliver massive blast overpressure more precisely on a target, grant the US a more significant hard-target-kill capability against hardened silos and C^3 facilities.[15] The super-hardened structure of Russian-built silos, and the fact that any such counter-force strike would assuredly be in the context of a general outbreak of hostilities (either international or inadvertent), would eliminate the collateral-damage concerns that plague defence planners in more limited 'bunker-busting' strike scenarios against rogue states. The American force may become quantitatively smaller in the years ahead, but *qualitative* improvements will further transform this force into a robust and highly lethal 'silo-busting' arsenal.

The US land-based force of 500 *Minuteman* III missiles is already highly accurate and the majority are armed with the high-yield W78 warhead.

However, the remaining low-yield W62 warheads will, under the Safety Enhanced Re-entry Vehicle programme, be replaced by an estimated 200 high-yield MX W87 warheads. Accuracy is continuing to be improved with an ongoing multi-phase $6–7bn modernisation programme that will provide, among other things, the more sophisticated N-50 guidance system. In addition to these planned upgrades, the concept of a modified *Minuteman* Elite force with much-improved guidance and targeting capabilities is currently being circulated among defence planners.[16] Modernisation plans also promise to improve the American sea-based strategic forces, which in 2008 – after the retirement of the last *Trident* I C-4 missile – will be composed of 336 highly accurate D-5 SLBMs armed with 2,000 W76 and W88 warheads. The 400 W88 are especially viable silo-busters, in that they are capable of similar yields (up to 475 kilotonnes) as the MX warhead. This sea-based force will also be the subject of a number of modernisation programmes, which will upgrade both the missiles' Mk-6 guidance system for a smaller CEP and the W76 warhead for a ground-burst capability that would make these warheads employable in silo-busting missions. Moreover, the United States seems to be interested in giving the missile's re-entry vehicle both global-positioning system accuracy and manoeuvrability, which together would greatly improve the feasibility of launching these missiles in a depressed trajectory. This appears to have been the goal of the most recent *Trident* II D-5 missile test in March 2005, as part of the now-cancelled Enhanced Effectiveness programme. But current proposals to use this manoeuvrable-re-entry-vehicle (MARV) technology on conventional SLBMs, as part of the Conventional *Trident* Modification (CTM) programme, should be equally transferable to the nuclear *Trident* arsenal.[17] Even the manned penetrator bomber force is undergoing modernisation, with the service-life extensions for the ALCM and the advanced cruise missile (ACM), and the addition of more 'low-observable' technology to the stealthy B-2 bombers. The 2006 QDR details plans to retire 38 nuclear-capable B-52s and to use the savings to modernise more fully the B-2 and other global-strike platforms, but Congress argued the need to maintain these bombers until a replacement capability was developed and, therefore, successfully blocked this initiative.[18]

Expanded targeting requirements provide an important rationale for the current fixation on *new* counter-force capabilities. Firstly, the US has to develop and maintain the capability to hold at risk the growing number of HDBTs. The 2001 *Report to Congress on the Defeat of Hardened and Deeply Buried Targets* defined HDBTs as structures that varied 'from hardened surface bunker complexes to deep tunnels' that can be used by adversaries to protect strategic and tactical assets, including: C^3 and leadership facilities;

'production, assembly, storage and deployment facilities' for WMD; facilities for artillery or missile-launchers; and air or area-defence systems.[19] The US estimates that there are over 10,000 HDBTs worldwide and that this number will no doubt increase. Tactical facilities are suspected to be hidden in shallow 'cut-and-cover' designs, which would be vulnerable to current or developmental weapons. However, it is estimated that the most threatening strategic facilities (e.g. leadership, C^3, WMD) would likely be protected in 1,400 particularly hardened HDBTs that are located near urban areas. Conventional weapons may not have sufficient destructive capabilities, while the silo-busting capabilities of the existing high-yield nuclear arsenal would be seen as producing excessive collateral damage in a disarming but otherwise limited (e.g. 'single weapon') counter-force strike against an HDBT on rogue-state territory.[20]

Secondly, the United States has placed a renewed emphasis on developing capabilities that can destroy or neutralise CB agents. These facilities are suspected to be housed in HDBTs, but the physical destruction of the target is not enough if CB agents remain 'viable or [are] released into the environment', with potentially catastrophic effects on nearby urban populations.[21] Collateral damage, either through the strike itself or the accidental dispersal of the CB agents, is, therefore, seen as an important concern of this target requirement. For that reason, new capabilities are needed to identify agent-production and storage facilities, and to deny access to, immobilise, neutralise or destroy such agents. Nuclear weapons are perceived to have potentially useful agent-defeat capabilities, in that their high heat and radiation levels could incinerate CB agents. Any nuclear ADWs would, however, require extensive modifications to reduce the yield in order to minimise collateral damage and radioactive fallout.

Thirdly, American strategic forces are compelled to track and destroy mobile and relocatable targets (MRTs). These targets can include such strategic assets as ballistic- or cruise-missile launchers, CB weapons and production facilities, and C^3 systems that are either movable (e.g. relocatable targets) or are on rail-, road- or ship-mobile platforms (e.g. mobile targets). The very mobility of these targets places a premium on intelligence, surveillance and reconnaissance (ISR) capabilities. These targets are neither hardened nor difficult to destroy using conventional weapons, provided that the United States has sufficient ISR and precision-guided strike capabilities to identify, track and engage an MRT target.[22] Nuclear weapons do, however, provide a greater assurance that the target will be destroyed, in the event that the target is either especially threatening or, given the larger radius of destruction, if its location is not precisely identified.[23]

The new triad places a premium on the development of new capabilities to fulfil these expanded targeting requirements. Conventional weapons are seen as being a potentially useful means of holding these targets at risk and, if necessary, of destroying them without the excessive collateral damage and stigma of a nuclear strike. Indeed, attention may have followed the Bush administration's controversial fascination with a nuclear response to HDBTs, but the Pentagon has equally been focused on developing a new generation of conventional bunker-busters. Active kinetic penetration, such as the US Army's 'Deep Digger' project, promises to increase feasible penetration depth through new tunnelling technology, while the 'small-diameter bomb' would allow a number of these weapons to neutralise a dispersed target and thus partly addressing the problem of the smaller radius of destruction inherent in conventional weaponry.[24] Hard Target Smart Fuse technology, which would allow a detonation to be controlled for optimal ground-shock effectiveness, has already been used to augment the BLU-116 Advanced Unitary Penetrator, one of the newest conventional EPWs in the American arsenal.[25] In addition, the US is currently developing low-blast high-fragmentation weapons that could be tailored to release CB agents from their storage containers, at which point some form of chemical neutralisation and/or high-temperature incendiary neutralisation, possibly through fuel-air explosives and thermobaric weapons, could take place.[26] Mobile targets remain the most vulnerable target requirement to non-nuclear offensive capabilities, as it is more a question of intelligence and tracking rather than new-kill capabilities. But the emphasis on conventional long-range strike capabilities, evident in the current plan to place conventional payloads on a limited number of SLBMs as part of the CTM, does promise to increase the American ability to destroy these targets promptly.[27]

The NPR states that 'the addition of non-nuclear strike forces … means that the US will be less dependent than it has been in the past on nuclear forces to provide its offensive deterrent capability'.[28] That being said, the United States also notes the limitations of using non-nuclear strike systems to target and destroy HDBTs or CB agents. Conventional weapons can only 'deny' or 'disrupt' the functioning of HDBTs, and 'are not effective for the long term physical destruction of deep, underground facilities'.[29] Nuclear weapons, on the other hand, are seen as having a greater ability to destroy underground targets through ground shock, and can neutralise and destroy CB agents through incineration and irradiation. The aforementioned 2001 report to Congress on HDBT states that: 'Nuclear weapons have a unique ability to destroy both agent containers and CBW [chemical-

and biological-weapon] agents', though one should qualify this remark by noting the continuing questions on whether a nuclear EPW could reduce collateral damage owing to fallout.[30]

However, the current arsenal of nuclear weapons is also considered to have a limited capability to hold strategic HDBTs at risk. For example, while the B61-11 weapon combines both earth-penetration and a 'dial-a-yield' system (which gives it the potential for a yield lower than one kilotonne), it is still considered a non-precise weapon that 'cannot survive penetration into many types of terrain in which hardened underground facilities are located'.[31] The new triad, therefore, advocates the development of a more effective EPW that would be able to generate sufficient ground shock to hold HDBTs at risk. The Robust Nuclear Earth Penetrator (RNEP) project was a study on the feasibility and cost of modifying an existing nuclear weapon (the two candidates being the B-61 and the B-83) to obtain an earth-penetration capability, while other Advanced Concepts Initiative (ACI) projects examined concepts for new warhead designs. New weapons would be tailored to threaten credibly a number of an adversary's key military assets and, as such, could be potentially useful for both tactical, battlefield missions and for the strategic purpose of deterrence by denial. These projects were blocked and effectively terminated by Congress in 2005 and 2006 but there are continuing concerns that work on new nuclear capabilities has simply shifted to more ambiguous projects.

The American search for more flexible and adaptive nuclear-war plans, which is seen as key to defeating both HDBTs and MRTs identified in the NPR's new targeting requirements, has also accelerated under the Bush administration. The SWPS, which has already undergone an expensive upgrade throughout most of the 1990s, was the object of a SWPS Transformation Study beginning in 2002 that examined the responsiveness of the system for flexible planning. This system will undergo a subsequent modernisation plan – SWPS-M, later renamed the Integrated Strategic Planning and Analysis Network – that seeks to utilise computer models to develop a streamlined, net-centric and more adaptive nuclear-planning system.

American nuclear-war-planning itself has also undergone some changes in recent years. The traditionally inflexible SIOP, which was most recently released as SIOP-03 in 2003, was subsequently renamed Operations Plan 8044 (OPLAN-8044). In some respects, this deliberative plan for 'anticipated contingencies' has continued the longstanding US emphasis on counter-force targeting of Russia and China, including counter-C^3 and counter-leadership targeting.[32] As noted in the most recent

NUWEP, issued in April 2004, American strategic forces would be used to threaten the destruction of 'those critical war-making and war-supporting assets and capabilities that a potential enemy leadership values most and that it would rely on to achieve its own objectives in a post-war world'.[33] This emphasis on destroying 'war-making and war-supporting' capabilities, which would combine an emphasis on such strategic assets as WMD and C^3 with an unknown number of critical economic targets, is justified on the basis that an adversary places greater 'value' on military capabilities as opposed to its own citizens. Denial of military capabilities for aggression would better enable deterrence than societal or population targeting.

Deliberative planning would, however, be joined with a new set of adaptive and crisis action plans. The United States has a long-standing interest in improving its adaptive planning capabilities. This would allow the US rapidly to generate limited nuclear-war plans, based on the targeting options developed for the deliberative plan, for a number of potential contingencies. Crisis action planning seeks to provide a prompt-strike capability, from minutes to hours, in totally unexpected contingencies. This type of planning has already been codified in CONPLAN-8022 and is a component of the administration's emphasis on 'global strike', which, according to reports of a classified 2003 directive, entails 'precision kinetic (nuclear and conventional) and non-kinetic (elements of space and information operations)' in support of American objectives.[34] This type of prompt-strike planning seems to denote implicitly a nuclear pre-emptive posture, or at the very least makes such a posture more feasible. Global strike has already been assigned as a new responsibility for STRATCOM, which, when placed alongside other strategic-mission assignments, represents a dramatic expansion of the command's authority.[35] With an 'Interim Global Strike Alert Order' approved in 2004 and the creation of a Space and Global Strike Functional Component Command at STRATCOM, it appears that prompt global strike is becoming a central new mission for American strategic forces.

Active and passive defences

The new-triad strategy explicitly incorporates defences as an integral component of the American strategic nuclear posture. This signifies recognition that nuclear weapons, even with new counter-force capabilities and integrated with advanced non-nuclear options, may not be sufficient for current deterrence requirements. According to NSPD-23 on *National Policy on Ballistic Missile Defence*, adversaries are perceived as having potential 'risk-prone' leaders who see WMD 'as weapons of choice, not of last resort'.[36] This not only raises the spectre of irrational or undeterrable rogue states, but also of coldly ambitious powers that would readily brandish these weapons as tools of coercion, compellence and blackmail. Defences would, however, be capable of denying or at least reducing the strategic or military utility of these weapons. As the NPR clearly notes, with the reinforcement of deterrence there would be an 'insurance against the failure of traditional deterrence'.[37]

Both passive and active defences are highlighted in the 2002 NPR. Passive defences constitute measures that would 'reduce the probability of and minimise the effects of damage caused by a hostile action without the intention of taking the initiative'.[38] The United States can instigate a number of measures, including hardening, concealment and mobility, to reduce the vulnerability of its military forces against an adversary's counter-force strike. These could be complemented by passive measures to reduce the damage of a successful strike, which would be useful not only to protect American forces but also to shield civilians from counter-value strikes or catastrophic terrorist attacks. A capacity to undertake area decontamination and mass vaccinations, alongside a military capability to operate in a WMD environment, would be only some of the many measures required for effective consequence management. The cost effectiveness of civil defence would, in contrast to the Cold War, also make this a potentially attractive option.[39]

Active defence measures can be defined as 'the employment of limited offensive action and counter-attacks to deny a contested area or position to the enemy'.[40] Air defences are the most prevalent form of active defence and have been used for many decades to deny an adversary control over a country's airspace. Missile defences are the more recent and controversial variant of an active-defence system. Despite acknowledging the importance of both active- and passive-defence measures, the difference in their respective emphasis in the NPR is striking. Mentions of passive defences are brief and devoid of detail, while a global BMD system is singled out for discussion. Various active and passive measures may be under development, but global missile defence clearly has a privileged position as the second leg of the new triad.

The Clinton administration, while keen to develop TMD to protect forward-deployed forces and American allies, had only grudgingly moved towards NMD deployments. In contrast, Bush had – even as a presidential candidate – clearly shown his enthusiasm for the missile-defence project and moved quickly to put his own stamp on previous efforts. On 1 May 2001, Bush stated that he would examine 'all available technologies and basing modes for effective missile defenses', and raised the possibility of 'near-term options' that would allow 'an initial capability against limited threats'. [41] A new strategic framework to replace the ABM Treaty was also highlighted. Similar remarks would be made by a number of senior Bush administration officials, including Deputy Secretary of Defense Paul Wolfowitz and Lieutenant-General Ronald Kadish, head of the Ballistic Missile Defense Organization (BMDO), during Congressional testimony in the summer of 2001, in an apparent effort to gain support for the administration's missile-defence plans.

A gradual unveiling of the Bush administration's approach to missile defence would follow. Firstly, the divide between TMD and NMD would be eliminated, as the administration argued that such a distinction was based on the archaic ABM Treaty and did not reflect the fact that 'theatre' and 'national' systems can potentially be tested and used interchangeably.[42] The administration envisions a global and multi-layered missile-defence system that would be capable of protecting the continental United States, as well as its deployed forces and allies, against an adversary's ballistic-missile attack in all phases of its flight trajectory. Boost-phase interception would target the missile after its launch and before it reaches the atmosphere, when counter-measures have yet to be deployed and its heat signature is most visible. If any warheads were not rendered inoperable at this stage, a midcourse-phase interceptor would attempt to recognise any deployed counter-measures and hit the warhead in space. The last layer, and the one that leaves the least room for error, is the terminal phase of the interception. Fortunately, many of the decoys and chaff counter-measures, and other penetration aids would at this point be filtered by re-entry into the atmosphere. A multi-layered approach has the potential advantage of multiplying the chances of a successful interception, though questions remain as to whether failure of the first layer could lead to the saturation of subsequent layers.[43]

Secondly, missile defence would undergo a number of organisational and procedural changes that would accelerate the deployment date for these systems. In 2001, the BMDO lost its authority over deployment, and focused solely on research and development programmes – this organisation would subsequently be renamed the Missile Defense Agency. In order to aid early (some would say premature) missile-defence deployments, the Pentagon would procure these systems using an approach known as 'capability-based acquisition', which places the emphasis on the rapid deployment of capabilities – even if insufficiently tested – rather than the deployment of platforms that have fulfilled military requirements. The majority of missile-defence systems have only undergone developmental testing in a manufactured and controlled environment, rather than operational testing in a realistic environment, yet this approach would still allow the Bush administration to begin to deploy initial capabilities of otherwise immature technology. Furthermore, given that any global BMD capability would require a host of different missile-defence systems, the Pentagon's use of a 'spiral development' or 'evolutionary acquisition' model means this initial capability – which could have some marginal deterrent value – could be augmented by various BMD capabilities as they become available.[44]

The 2002 NPR placed the onus on the acquisition of 'near-term emergency capabilities', and the Bush administration appears to have wasted little time in securing just such a system. Missile defence received nearly $8.2bn for 2002, which was a $3bn increase from the previous year and represented the highest spending for this project since 1993.[45] Nearly half of these funds were directed at two BMD components: the Ground-based Midcourse Defence (GMD) and Sea-based Midcourse Defense (SMD) programmes, which are the follow-ups to Clinton's plans for a NMD and a NTW system respectively. The budget did not openly specify any funds for initial deployments, though funds were secured to develop an expanded Missile Defense Test Bed that was justified on the need to undertake more realistic test conditions. However, this test bed would entail not only an expansion of existing ground-based interceptors (GBIs) at the testing facility on Kodiak Island, Alaska, but also a number of changes that were more useful for operational missile-defence deployments – this included five GBIs at a new facility in Fort Greely, Alaska, an upgrade to the *Cobra Dane* radar on Shemya Island, as well as improvements to early-warning systems and Battle Management Command and Control nodes at various locations.[46]

Any ambiguity in the administration's plans would end on 13 December 2001, as the Bush administration finally announced its intention to withdraw from the ABM Treaty six months later. Further details of the plans for an initial BMD deployment were noted in the subsequent leak of the NPR, which suggested a number of potential options to provide this emergency capability:

- A single ABL for boost-phase intercepts may be available for limited operations against ballistic missiles of all ranges;
- A rudimentary ground-based midcourse system, consisting of a small number of interceptors taken from the test programme and an upgraded *Cobra Dane* radar in Alaska against longer-range threats, could be available against longer-range threats to the United States;
- A sea-based *Aegis* system could be available to provide rudimentary midcourse capability against short- to medium-range threats.[47]

The end state of the missile-defence architecture is not highlighted in the NPR and, indeed, will likely never be announced due to the spiral-development nature of the current system. But the document does foresee that the emergency BMD system capability for 2006–09 would consist of up to three ABL aircraft, additional GMD sites, four SMD ships, and terminal systems like the PAC-3 and THAAD.[48] NSPD-23 expanded on these details by noting the need to reach an agreement with the United Kingdom and Denmark on the upgrade to early-warning radars in Fylingdales and Thule, Greenland (which would be signed in 2003 and 2004 respectively), as well as the possible evolution of the BMD system to include space-based defences.[49] In December 2002, the Bush administration publicly announced a specific plan to field an initial missile-defence capability by 2004, including: 16 GBIs at Fort Greely, Alaska, and four GBIs at Vandenberg Air Force Base, California, against long-range missile threats; 20 interceptors on three ships against short- and intermediate-range missiles; and an unknown quantity of PAC-3 terminal-phase interceptors.

Funding has continued to increase significantly since the Bush administration took office. From a little over $7bn in 2003, it would achieve an impressive $9bn in 2004 and $10bn in 2005. The majority of these funds would be spent on near-term projects, such as the current plan to field sea- and land-based interceptors and PAC-3s, rather than the more exotic laser technology in the ABL and Space-based Laser (SBL). The budget was reduced slightly to $8bn in 2006. However, the Bush administration's budget request for 2007 totalled over $11bn, with nearly $3bn going to the GMD system and $1bn going to both the *Aegis* Ballistic Missile Defense System (ABMDS), formerly known as the SMD system, and the THAAD terminal-phase system.[50]

As of 2006, American strategic-defence capabilities consisted of eight GBIs in Alaska and two GBIs in California, with ten SM-3 interceptors for the ABMDS reportedly been delivered to two ships.[51] There are, however, continuing questions as to the reliability of a GMD system against long-range missiles that has only had a dubious record during developmental testing and, with the addition of a new booster rocket, has yet to be tested in its current deployed configuration. In contrast, the sea-based ABMDS is a midcourse-phase missile-defence system designed to protect American overseas deployments against theatre-range ballistic missiles. But owing to its relatively high success rate and promising technology, based on the already existent ABMDS, the programme has been expanded to study the possible use of this system in boost-phase intercepts, as well as against any long-range ICBM attack. These strategic defences have also been complemented by the PAC-3 tactical-defence system, which is designed for terminal-phase defence against short-range theatre missiles. This system remains the most tested and successful of American active defences, though with some reservations about its efficacy during the 2003 Iraq War.

In the budget request for 2007, the Bush administration predicts that by 2007 there will be 20 GBIs deployed in Alaska (alongside the two already deployed in California), 24 SM-3 interceptors for the ABMDS and a total of 534 interceptors for the PAC-3 tactical-defence system.[52] This will likely be augmented in the future with a number of boost- and terminal-phase capabilities. The ABL, while plagued by a host of technological and operational issues, and only lukewarm support from Congress, might be fielded as a boost-phase interceptor. The SBL could be further developed if the United States begins to implement, rather than merely discuss, a policy of space dominance. Cooperative ventures with allies on missile defence, of which the MEADS programme to develop an air and missile-defence system with France and Germany is the most pertinent demonstration, are likely to proliferate as a means to offset costs, to gain political support and to prevent any sense of a strategic American decoupling from its allies.[53] A terminal-phase theatre-defence capability could be provided by the THAAD system, which is designed to intercept short- and medium-range missiles, and could potentially be modified to intercept long-range missiles. Existing tracking sensors would be greatly improved with the development of a massive X-band radar, which will be located on a semi-submersible sea-based platform. More controversial is the plan to develop the Space Tracking and Surveillance System (STSS), which is a constellation of low-earth-orbit satellite systems that would be used to track and discriminate between warheads and penetration aids. The STSS, which is a component of the larger Space-Based Infrared System programme, has been over budget and – due to the spiral-development model – will likely not be sufficiently tested prior to initial deployment.[54]

The second leg of the new triad remains somewhat paradoxical. On the one hand, despite the fervour of the Bush administration to deploy and integrate strategic defences alongside American offensive-strike systems, it appears that any missile-defence system will – for at least the next few years – be quite modest and limited. Contrary to pledges to explore new options, the Bush administration also appears simply to have increased funding, with only minor modifications, for the existing number of active defence programmes. On the other hand, the Bush administration has also been highly circumspect regarding the long-term architecture of any eventual missile-defence system. This might be necessitated by the spiral-development model of procurement, but it also hides the total cost of the BMD programme and makes it easy to question whether the underlying intention is eventually to deploy a thick and robust missile-defence shield. Indeed, the sheer number of missile-defence programmes, and the evident intention to use ambitious theatre-based defences like THAAD and ABMDS to protect the continental United States homeland, 'implies deploying at least a thousand interceptors capable of long-range defense'.[55] This would represent a significant strategic-defence capability for the American homeland and, with the addition of tactical and theatre-defence systems, the total deployment vision could entail as many as 2,000 interceptors. Even this number could expand as technology continues to advance, and if such long-term and exotic projects as SBL become prioritised. Technological immaturity and the Pentagon's willingness to begin deployment of still-untested interceptors has led defence analyst Kurt Guthe to label it 'the most uncertain part of the new triad'.[56] But the gradual and evolutionary nature of missile-defence deployments should not obscure the long-term ambition of this approach.

Responsive nuclear infrastructure

The new triad's vision of a seamless war-fighting capability, including the deployment of new nuclear and conventional long-range strike forces alongside a complex and integrated array of diverse missile-defence systems, is an ambitious manifestation of the Pentagon's interest in military 'transformation'. It is also meant to ensure the continued long-term viability of American strategic primacy. However, the technological hurdles to realising this vision are significant, even for a country with as impressive a technological edge as the United States. The current strategic arsenal not only has to be maintained, with its elements' service life extended and qualitative improvements implemented to the delivery system and warhead components, but the American ability to undertake research into new nuclear capabilities, alongside conventional offensive-strike and missile-defence technology, must also be revitalised and accelerated. To better provide the foundation for such a transformation, the NPR has placed the need for a responsive defence infrastructure in an especially privileged position as the third leg of the new triad.

The NPR states that the American defence infrastructure has contracted, and emphasises the need for new approaches to development and procurement 'so that it will not take 20 years or more to field new generations of weapon systems'.[57] One may surmise that the capabilities-based acquisition model of procurement, which is currently being applied to the development of missile defence, represents one of these new measures to accelerate the deployment of new capabilities. This leg may represent an overarching concept to provide the means for the transformation of both nuclear and non-nuclear capabilities alike, as befitting the expanded nature of the new-triad strategic posture. Yet the need to revitalise the nuclear infrastructure is given particular attention in the NPR. This is perhaps not surprising, given the fact that strategic nuclear weapons have a central and unique role in the new triad strategy itself, alongside continuing concerns as to the long-term safety and reliability of the existing nuclear arsenal, not to mention the atrophied US ability to develop new nuclear capabilities in the post-Cold War period. The American nuclear-weapons complex had shrunk quite significantly in the aftermath of the Cold War. Not only did it have to deal with the cancellation of future weapon systems (such as the Small ICBM) and the curtailment of its role in designing new weapons, but also a nuclear-testing moratorium that made even its ability to assure (or certify) the safety and reliability of the existing arsenal problematic.

Concerns were partially alleviated with the creation of the multi-billion-dollar Stockpile Stewardship Program (SSP) in 1994. Instead of empirical nuclear testing, the SSP relied on sophisticated computers, small-scale laboratories and large-scale experimental facilities that, by using the data from the long history of American nuclear tests, would be able to simulate nuclear testing.[58] The reliability of the existing arsenal would be monitored through an Enhanced Surveillance Program. In the event that any problems were detected, many of the components could be replaced through a Life Extension Program (LEP). However, this programme did not address the continued erosion of the American nuclear-weapon design and production capabilities. The LEP would be able to replace a number of components, but its ability to replace the nuclear-explosive package of the warhead was limited by both the nuclear-testing moratorium and the inability to furnish new warhead components. Instead, only original or very similar components were used as replacements and any changes had to be kept to a minimum.

The new triad's emphasis on a responsive nuclear infrastructure is meant to forestall two potential problems that, according to the NPR, could result from the dilapidated nuclear-weapons production complex. On the one hand, the inability to build nuclear warheads, including such critical components as the plutonium pits, could pose a danger in the event that a serious problem is discovered in an existing warhead. The current reliance on the LEP, and its limited approach in maintaining the nuclear-explosive package of the warhead, means that the United States might simply be unable to cope with just such an eventuality. As such, the long-term reliability of an increasingly ageing strategic arsenal, which was never intentionally designed to be maintained for decades after its original service life, could be questioned. On the other hand, the current approach towards maintaining the nuclear arsenal, at the expense of nuclear-weapon development and production, limits American options for dealing with future threat scenarios that might require new nuclear capabilities. This problem was presaged in the extended-targeting requirements of the offensive-strike leg of the new triad. As the NPR notes, a responsive nuclear infrastructure should be able to 'design, develop, manufacture and certify new warheads in response to new national requirements'.[59]

Both challenges require an increased capability to produce nuclear warheads and a readiness to undertake empirical testing, though the need to produce new nuclear capabilities would entail an attendant emphasis on formulating new nuclear-weapon designs. The NNSA took little time in implementing the NPR's guidance for a responsive nuclear infrastructure. On 22 April 2003, the Los Alamos National Laboratory announced the creation of the first plutonium pit since the closure of Rocky Flats, Colorado in 1989. This represented an interim pit-production facility, which was expected to be joined by the more ambitious Modern Pit Facility (MPF) capable of producing between 125 and 450 pits annually. The MPF is estimated to cost $2–4bn in construction and up to $300m in annual maintenance.[60] The Bush administration has also been keen reduce the readiness time for nuclear testing, down from its current 24–36 months to 18 months. The need for empirical nuclear testing has been supported by comments by Dale Klein, the assistant to Donald Rumsfeld for nuclear, chemical and biological defence programmes, and has been reiterated in a two-page memorandum circulated to members of the NWC by E.C. Aldridge Jr, former undersecretary of defense for acquisition, technology and logistics, that advocates an assessment of the technical risks associated with maintaining the US nuclear arsenal without testing.[61] The Nevada Test Site (NTS), which is currently limited to undertaking sub-critical testing, is the focus for these efforts under the Enhanced Readiness Program. The SSP has, not surprisingly, also seen impressive annual increases in funding that currently total $6.4bn annually.[62]

Both the MPF and the NTS activity have, however, raised continuing questions from a Congress that has been quite sceptical of the need for either a large pit-production capability, given the modest facility already installed at Los Alamos, or a reduction in nuclear-testing readiness. As a result, the MPF has had problems securing even the relatively modest funding requests for its initial developments. Funding was cut to $10.8m in 2004 and $7m in 2005 (as compared to requests of $22.8m and $30m respectively), while no funds were appropriated for 2006. In the FY2007 budget request, the administration appears to have temporarily suspended funding for this project. Funding for the NTS has followed a similar pattern. While the total request of $24.9m was successfully appropriated in 2004, funding would begin to be reduced in 2005 ($30m request and $22.5m appropriated). But alongside the MPF, funding would be totally rejected in the 2006 budget, with Congress noting that existing problems at the NTS meant that 24 months was the lowest achievable state of test readiness, and would be conspicuously absent in the FY2007 budget request.[63]

Equally, controversy has plagued the Bush administration's plans to develop the foundations for new nuclear capabilities. The ACI was the centrepiece of these efforts. Small advance-concept teams, which had been eliminated in the post-Cold War period, would be developed in each of the nuclear-weapon laboratories as well as Washington DC. While stockpile maintenance would continue to be the key rationale of the nuclear-weapons infrastructure, these teams would provide an initial capability to undertake nuclear-weapon design and capability studies. Concepts that were considered to be useful included: modifications for increased yield flexibility; improved earth-penetration capabilities; and warheads that were compatible with reduced collateral-damage requirements.[64] As part of this initiative, the Air Force had undertaken concept studies on the modification of a warhead, while the Lawrence Livermore National Laboratory had examined the possibility of designing and tailoring nuclear-weapon effects.[65] The majority of funding for the initiative has, however, gone to the RNEP project. These projects would provide a chance to redevelop the intellectual capital necessary for a reinvigorated warhead infrastructure. Information from these projects, while not openly directed at developing a 'mini-nuke', would certainly have applicability to such a project. The new targeting requirements and renewed emphasis on limiting collateral damage do provide a rationale for the need to develop low-yield and more usable nuclear warheads. Such a development might still be too controversial at the moment, yet future intentions on this issue remain quite ambiguous. With the successful repeal of the Spratt–Furse ban on mini-nuke research, it appears that the foundations for the future development of mini-nukes are slowly being laid.

While still fully funded in 2003, Congressional concerns about the RNEP study would reduce the $15m request to $7.5m in 2004, which would only be channelled to the B-83 project. The other ACI projects had their request for $6m approved, though the majority of funds would only be released pending a stockpile report. The ACI suffered an even more damaging setback in 2005, as Congress cut funding for the RNEP project due to questions regarding a five-year budget projection that prepared for RNEP development and totalled nearly $485m, while the $9m request for other ACI projects was redirected towards the Congressionally authorised Reliable Replacement Warhead (RRW) programme. This effectively marked the temporary end of the ACI project. In 2006, the RNEP did not receive any appropriations for its modest $8.5m budget request, though partial funding was authorised to study a conventional-penetrator test. The RRW, on the other hand, received appropriations totalling $25m. The RNEP did not even appear in the 2007 budget request.[66]

The RRW represents a movement away from the refurbishment of nuclear warheads based on minimal changes to the warhead components, to the replacement of existing warheads that are easier to manufacture and certify without nuclear testing. On the one hand, this programme can be seen as a Congressionally authorised defeat of the Bush administration's ambitions to develop new nuclear capabilities. After all, the RRW is meant to increase stockpile reliability, but without any movement towards new nuclear-weapon designs or warhead capabilities. On the other hand, the NNSA has clearly embraced the possibility of a more reliable and safer means of replacing nuclear warheads. The May 2005 report, entitled *Sustaining the Nuclear Enterprise: A New Approach*, argued for precisely such a sustainable approach to replace the existing SSP.[67] It is true that the RRW's policy would lead to the creation of new nuclear components and safer nuclear-warhead designs that would be used to replace warheads in the existing arsenal of nuclear weapons. This could, in turn, lead to reductions in the reserve stockpile, as more reliable warheads would lessen the need for reserve warheads to act as replacements, and greater certifiability that would lessen future requirements for nuclear testing. Yet there are continuing questions as to whether this programme will simply provide 'a back door for the administration to circumvent congressional opposition to new warhead designs for new and destabilising nuclear strike missions'.[68] After all, an implicit assumption of the RRW is that yield could be traded in return for increased warhead safety, which would provide at least the technical capability to undertake modifications to the existing arsenal.

The RRW represents a potentially new direction for the SSP and, despite its Congressional origins, has become a key component of the Bush administration's vision for a responsive nuclear infrastructure. According to the 2005 Nuclear Weapons Project Task Force (NWPTF) report, entitled *Recommendations for the Nuclear Weapons Complex of the*

Future (also known as the Overskei Report), the current American nuclear infrastructure is neither productive nor responsive, and remains reliant on early Cold War-era production facilities that fail to meet even current refurbishment requirements. This task force envisions a complex that in 2030 would be capable of the automated annual production 125 'new' weapons and the dismantling of 125 stockpile weapons, and a responsiveness to meet new security requirements – such as 48 months to design and produce a new nuclear weapon and 18 months to resume nuclear testing. The NWPTF recommends not only the immediate production of the RRW, but also the dismantling of the Cold War stockpile at the Pantex and Y-12 facilities, and the consolidation of all nuclear-explosive package production, assembly and dismantling activities into a single Consolidated Nuclear Production Centre.[69] At this point, it remains unclear whether a Congress that has become increasingly sceptical of the Bush administration's nuclear-weapon proposals will fund the RRW, and indeed the other recommendations of the NWPTF.

CHAPTER FOUR

'Nuclear Superiority' and the Dilemmas for Strategic Stability

The new triad envisions a future strategic posture based on an array of sophisticated counter-force capabilities, spearheaded by the American nuclear arsenal and supported by conventional offensive and defensive systems. The central goal of the new triad is the successful dissuasion and/or deterrence of a rogue state armed with WMD, and if necessary, its decisive and damage-limiting defeat in the event of deterrence failure. The strategy underlying the new triad vision, which links the posture's means to these political ends, is explicitly based on the counter-force targeting of a rogue state's strategic military capabilities. The United States would obtain the ability to control any form of escalation with and deny any WMD deterrence capability from these asymmetrical regional adversaries.

At a more implicit level, this strategy would also translate these denial and escalation-dominance capabilities for use against more formidable potential peer competitors such as Russia and China. It might be an overstatement to consider the outcome to be a splendid first-strike capability that would be able to prevent any significant Russian retaliation, but at the very least the United States could obtain a critical 'assured-destruction edge' against the strategic capabilities of both established nuclear powers for the foreseeable future.

The theme underlying the new triad strategy is the need to obtain 'full-spectrum dominance' against potential adversaries. As the NPR notes, the new triad would 'make it more arduous and costly for an adversary to compete militarily with or wage war against the United States'.[1] This primacist inclination was codified in the 2002 NSS, and is perfectly encapsulated by Bush's statement that 'America has, and intends to keep, military strengths beyond challenge'.[2] A strategy to extend the 'unipolar moment' indefinitely has now come into ascendance and displaced more restrained grand-strategy options. As noted by the American strategist Barry Posen, 'the new debate on US grand strategy is essentially about which variant of a hegemonic strategy the United States should pursue'.[3] 'Strategic fatigue' may have sapped the vitality from the Bush administration's policies, but this 'imperial over-reach' has only sharpened the debate on the modalities of a hegemonic strategy, specifically between the nationalistic and unilateral vision of the Bush administration and the multilateral and liberal vision that would likely be consolidated under the Democrats.[4] Over a decade after the release of the controversial 1992 Defense Planning Guidance, primacy finally became an openly acceptable grand-strategic vision in the White House.

The new triad strategy, if it is successfully implemented, represents a critical means of turning this grand-strategic vision into an enduring reality. Strategic superiority may indeed be directed at the immediate challenge of the motley collection of asymmetrical rogue states, yet at a time of such unchallenged American strategic dominance, it is equally tailored to the rising number of *potential* threats that, in an age of capability-based planning, have to be held at risk in today's 'target-rich environment'.[5] Such a strategy is highly ambitious in scope and will likely result in an ever-growing number of potential targets, or to use Wade Huntley's eloquent phrase 'threats all the way down', that need to be targeted for destruction.[6] Such an approach may be supported by a convincing strategic rationale based on the asymmetrical dangers that the United States, and indeed the international community, currently faces in the new security environment. But one should neither underestimate nor dismiss the consequences of this strategy. The resultant strategic destabilisation may be sufficiently severe to warrant, if not a radically altered approach to nuclear strategy, then at least a well-deserved reassessment and reformulation. Strategic stability offers a particularly useful means of assessing the new triad strategy. The counter-value logic of strategic stability was, however, largely formulated in the strategic context of the Cold War. In contrast, the new triad is a response to a transformed strategic-threat environment that is characterised not by a long-standing nuclear rivalry between two superpowers, but rather by a lone superpower that maintains a multiplicity of unstable adversarial relationships with various WMD-armed rogue-state proliferators, alongside more benign – but in the long term ambiguous – relationships with major nuclear powers. The premises underlying strategic stability, and indeed the counter-force arguments for deterrence credibility and failure that were more readily dismissed during the Cold War, deserve a reassessment in the current strategic context of the 'second nuclear age'.[7]

The strategic logic of the new triad

The new triad strategy represents the latest manifestation of the long-standing American trend towards nuclear revisionism. Rogue states may lack any semblance of the power projection and strategic depth of the Soviet Union. But these adversaries, due to this very imbalance of power, also pose a fundamental dilemma. The sheer disparity of power means that the United States can feasibly undertake military interventions against such adversaries. However, in the event that the US did have to intervene, there would be the potential that an adversary would use WMD, alongside traditional asymmetrical tools such as state-sponsored terrorism or insurgency, as a successful tool of deterrence. Such weapons could be brandished as a means of deterring the US from initiating any hostilities, as a form of intrawar deterrence to curtail American military objectives, or they could even be transferred to proxy forces or state-sponsored terrorist organisations.

The US would be placed in a difficult position for several reasons. On the one hand, the American ability to deter rogue states remains circumscribed. A rogue state's WMD deterrent capability will, at least in the near term, likely be based on CB weapons. Yet the elimination of the United States' CB stockpiles has effectively made nuclear weapons 'the only WMD available for retaliation'.[8] The highly destructive nature of nuclear weapons, when compared to chemical and, more debatably, biological weapons, raises the question of whether nuclear weapons are indeed a credible tool of deterrence and/or retaliation. Non-nuclear capabilities might seem to be a natural substitute, but conventional deterrence has traditionally been considered more ambiguous and prone to failure.[9] On the other hand, the United States faces a potential 'imbalance of resolve' with its rogue-state adversaries. This would be most acute during any regime-change campaign, which would threaten the existence of a rogue regime and leave little constraint on its behaviour. Mass-casualty WMD could be used in a last-ditch effort at intrawar deterrence, perhaps using a limited attack (and the promise of subsequent attacks) to compel an American military withdrawal, or simply as a 'Samson option' to exact revenge.[10] The United States might then find itself deterred from any such intervention or regime-change campaign.

It is true that the strategic deterrent capabilities of rogue states are very limited. With the possible exception of North Korea, most countries that have been stigmatised with the rogue-state label at one time or another – such as Iran, Syria, Libya and Iraq – were suspected of having only moderate amounts of CB agents and limited numbers of short- to medium-range delivery systems. Nuclear weapons have yet to proliferate to these countries, while intercontinental delivery systems have yet to be successfully tested and developed. However, these countries could still rely on asymmetrical means to deter the United States. Robert Harkavy uses the term 'triangular or indirect deterrence' to describe such a strategy:

> a weaker power lacking the capability to deter a stronger and (importantly) distant power, might choose to threaten a nuclear (or chemical or biological, or also conventional) riposte against a smaller, closer or contiguous state, usually but perhaps not always one allied to the larger tormentor or to one of its clients (or providing them basing access in a crisis), but perhaps also a neutral state, one with no real political connection to the ongoing conflict.[11]

According to this strategic logic, while the United States may be immune to a direct attack from a rogue state, it does have a number of critical assets and allies that could be held at risk of neutralisation or destruction. Regional allies, basing areas and troop deployments are quite vulnerable to the short- and medium-range capabilities of many regional adversaries. The US is an extra-regional power that remains heavily dependent on the use of forward-basing access for any intervention, and would be particularly exposed to such a threat.[12] The proliferation of both ballistic and cruise-missile technology also promises to increase both this 'triangular deterrence' capability and, in the future, the likelihood that rogue states will someday acquire delivery systems capable of reaching the continental United States.

The implications of such a situation are enormous. Rogue states would be able to use their limited WMD capabilities both to disrupt American deployments tactically and to deter the US by threatening its allies strategically. Regional allies, who would be the primary targets of any WMD retaliation, might be more accommodating of the rogue state's demands. At the very least, uncertainty over extended American security guarantees could lead to a proliferation cascade, as allies acquire WMD as a means of balancing the regional bully independently. The United States might effectively be immune to a direct attack in the short term, but as an extra-regional superpower, it might not be invested in any conflict to the degree of the rogue state, nor indeed compared to its regional allies.[13] In such a situation, 'the risks from involvement in a regional conflict are apt to escalate way beyond the prospective positive returns'.[14] This creates its own extended deterrence problems, as the United States might not find that the objectives of its military intervention to be important enough to warrant, for example, Iran or North Korea's devastating WMD retaliation on Riyadh, Tel Aviv or Tokyo. This problem would only be magnified in the future if a rogue state were to develop even a limited capability to attack the continental United States.[15]

The end result in such a scenario could very well be a de facto situation of MAD. Anathema to American nuclear planners during the Cold War, the re-creation of MAD meant that a risk-prone rogue-state adversary could potentially deter the United States and thereby protect the fruits of aggrandisement. Even if the US remained committed to intervening, such a situation could entail either a reassessment of its military objectives, in the event of a rogue state's attempt at intrawar deterrence, or a failure of deterrence that could lead to WMD use and American nuclear retaliation.

The new triad strategy is, foremost, a means of preventing a situation of de facto MAD from taking root and of mitigating the consequences of deterrence failure. New nuclear capabilities, rather than being designed purely for war-fighting or pre-emptive strikes, are meant to reinforce deterrence by making nuclear attacks more proportionate and credible against a rogue state's less destructive CB capabilities. Nuclear-bunker-busters and ADWs that can neutralise an adversary's HDBTs, C^3 facilities and WMD capabilities would reinforce American extended-deterrence guarantees. The balance of resolve in the conflict would shift in favour of the United States, which would be able to 'pursue its foreign policy interests more assertively'.[16] Perhaps more importantly, this deterrence-by-denial approach would make any retaliation more proportionate and more conducive to any strategic military objectives in the event of deterrence failure.

This emphasis on increasing the credibility of American nuclear capabilities does, however, also increase the military utility of these weapons and raises fears that they could be employed as tools for a pre-emptive strike against a rogue state.[17] This possibility should not be underestimated. In the midst of a regime-change campaign, when a rogue state might employ its own CB weapons, the perceived usability of nuclear EPWs and/or ADWs would increase the temptation – and lower the threshold – of a pre-emptive nuclear strike. This is likely the reason why a draft of the 2005 *Doctrine for Joint Nuclear Operations* (Joint Pub 3-12) outlines a number of pre-emptive theatre scenarios for nuclear use.[18] This document was admittedly cancelled due to the negative outcry over these scenarios. Indeed, one should not underestimate the height of the nuclear threshold or the potency of the nuclear taboo. However, with the implementation of crisis action planning (OPLAN-8066) that increasingly emphasises the rapid formulation and execution of limited nuclear strikes against these countries, the American capability – if not willingness – to undertake prompt, pre-emptive nuclear strikes has increased. Joint Pub 3-12 might officially have been cancelled, but the foundation for a pre-emptive *capability* has continued to be laid.

Conventional capabilities, both offensive and defensive, play an important role in this strategy. Nuclear weapons may be used as a means for pre-war deterrence of a rogue state's WMD use and, after the onset of hostilities, perhaps to attain some level of intrawar deterrence. But if the objectives are sufficiently ambitious, then these weapons may only be useful as a means of retaliation or pre-emption. New conventional counter-force weapons, such as conventional ballistic missiles and EPWs, would provide an entirely *usable* tool of counter-proliferation and allow the United States to undertake disarming strikes more freely during any conflict scenario. Tactical and TMD systems would reduce the likelihood of regional allies being successfully coerced by an aggressive WMD-armed rogue state, while strategic missile-defence systems would be a long-term project to delay such a de facto MAD situation from arising in a more serious way in the future. Active defences, however, become much more feasible after a first strike has already eliminated the majority of an adversary's offensive capabilities. In the event that a US pre-emptive counter-force attack – either conventional or, in an extreme situation, nuclear – is unable to disarm a rogue state's strategic deterrent fully, missile defence would provide a final safety net against any rogue state's residual retaliatory missile attacks. As noted in the 2005 *Doctrine for Joint Nuclear Operations*, such active defences allow for the employment of 'offensive counter-force strikes while enhancing security from catastrophic results if an adversary launches a retaliatory strike while under attack'.[19]

In this case, the combination of nuclear superiority and conventional primacy – tailored towards eliminating any asymmetrical advantages held by potential adversaries – will better enable the American power-projection capability to undertake regional military operations. Counter-force capabilities would more credibly threaten the strategic assets of rogue states and reinforce US regional deterrence of these adversaries. The United States would have a more tailored capability to control and dominate any escalatory threats made by a rogue state, irrespective of whether such threats are conventional, involve CB agents or even nuclear weapons. The United States might still, however, be confronted with a scenario where its nuclear capabilities would be insufficient for deterrence. Intrawar deterrence requires the ability to provide nuclear or other forms of deterrent signals that are visible even in the 'fog of war'. Moreover, the United States could have sufficiently ambitious military objectives so as to make deterrence failure inevitable. Escalation dominance against rogue states, therefore, entails obtaining satisfactory conditions for 'war termination' with the adversary, preferably with conventional weapons but not excluding nuclear use.

Nuclear counter-force capabilities that are designed for the escalation dominance of these strategically weak adversaries would, in turn, be equally usable against targets in such established nuclear-armed states as Russia and China. The expanded targeting requirements listed in the 2002 NPR are not, by any means, limited to rogue states. The challenges posed by HDBTs, and the need to develop earth-penetration capabilities as a solution, were a long-standing concern for American defence planners during the Cold War.[20] Yet the end of the Cold War neither eliminated these targets, nor the attendant American nuclear-war planners' desire to hold them at risk. Both Russia and China are suspected of having a large number of HDBTs capable of protecting their respective leadership and C^3 facilities. Good examples are the strategic HDBT facilities in the Yamantau and Kosvinsky mountains in Central and Southern Russia.[21] Earth-penetration capabilities designed against rogue states would, when combined with large-yield nuclear warheads, be potentially useful counter-force and decapitation weapons against these countries.

A similar argument could be made in the case of MRTs. Russia has long maintained a mobile component to its ICBM force which, given the large size of its relatively more vulnerable land-based systems, increases the survivability of its nuclear deterrent. As China begins to deploy solid-fuelled missiles, the temptation to further develop rail- or road-mobile ICBMs as a means of assuring the survival of China's relatively small arsenal will also likely increase. Moreover, the logic underpinning the MRT-targeting requirement is more closely associated with these scenarios. The central advantage of using a nuclear weapon against these targets, as opposed to a conventional weapon, is the high destructive radius of the blast. This reduces the need for precise intelligence, but entails an emphasis on high-yield weapons that would be unsuitable for a proportionate strike, with limited collateral damage, against a rogue state.[22] But given the inevitable scale of destruction of a major-power nuclear exchange, such weapons would be perfectly suitable in any US targeting of Russia or China.

The modernisation of American legacy nuclear systems also appears to be directed at these more formidable adversaries. Under the limits imposed by the Treaty of Moscow, these counter-force weapons will remain too numerous to be effectively justified against rogue states. As pointed out by Joseph Cirincione of the Carnegie Endowment for International Peace, 'there is no strategic justification for maintaining thousands of weapons on high alert and a reserve force of thousands more weapons ready for re-deployment other than to target Russia'.[23] Furthermore, strategic force-modernisation programmes promise to improve the accuracy and hard-target-kill capabilities of American land- and sea-based forces. While usable against HDBTs among rogue states, the growing inventory of high-yield warheads (such as the MX W87 and D-5 W88) appears more suitable for use against the hardened silos on Russian territory, as well as any silos that China may deploy in the future. As noted by political scientists Keir Lieber and Daryl Press, these 'nuclear programmes are hard to explain with any mission other than a nuclear first strike on a major power adversary'.[24]

Neither can the new triad's second leg, the development of global missile defence, be easily disentangled from this potential objective. A priority on TMD development would be the most logical approach to defending against a rogue-state attack. Short- and medium-range missiles are an immediate threat to American forces and allies in many of these regions, compared to the still-hypothetical intercontinental-range missile threat. Strategic defences might be a prudent long-term goal, but a limited active-defence system should be more than sufficient.[25] Yet the Bush administration, as modest as its initial GBI deployments may have been, has instead offered a much more ambitious and long-term vision of a thick strategic-defence system, as well as a variety of TMD systems that could potentially be compatible against long-range missiles. Such a robust commitment to strategic defence appears to be too large to be realistically justified by rogue states and raises questions as to the actual rationale for such a system. The continuing ambiguity on the end state of the proposed missile-defence architecture only increases Chinese and Russian concerns. Perhaps most ominously, such a system would only be capable of providing damage-limitation capabilities if a disarming first strike had already degraded Russia or China's respective arsenals. The strategic logic of thick 'area defences' becomes much more compelling when combined with a counter-force capability that, not incidentally, the United States has begun to reinvigorate.

The new triad strategy is being tailored to different kinds of potential adversaries. In scenarios involving rogue states, its goal is not simply to reinforce deterrence, but also to enable American power projection to defeat these adversaries. The nuclear superiority that is implicitly directed at potential major-power adversaries is far less ambitious, as the US has neither the inclination nor the capability to undertake military adventurism against either Russia or China. The United States would, however, obtain a critical strategic advantage against both countries. Given the dilapidated state of the Russian arsenal, and the small size of the Chinese arsenal, both countries would be even more vulnerable to an American disarming first strike. This would give the United States the ability to dominate any form of nuclear escalation by either country, with the attendant ability to initiate coercive threats more freely, and would be the culmination of decades of work by hawkish nuclear strategists to reverse the state of 'mutual' deterrence. Yet the different outcomes of this strategy remain informed by a fundamental *primacist* approach that, by seeking to obtain various political and military benefits from such strategic capabilities, represents a critical component of the drive towards grand-strategic primacy.

The future of strategic stability

The nuclear rivalry that developed between the US and the Soviet Union was defined by the idea of mutual vulnerability. A policy of MAD may have been rejected by American nuclear-war planners, and an attempt at attaining unilateral strategic advantage may have been initiated in its place, but the *reality* of the mutual vulnerability of both superpowers to a nuclear attack was much harder to dismiss.[26] The need to stabilise this nuclear rivalry, in order to prevent a catastrophic nuclear exchange, became a paramount concern. Other strategic considerations also played a role in the formulation of policy, with the most prominent being the need to threaten credibly a nuclear riposte against what the Soviet Union valued and to limit societal vulnerability in the event of a nuclear exchange. But the stability of the US–Soviet nuclear dyad, and the spectre of the consequences of instability, would be an ever-present preoccupation of nuclear strategists and policymakers throughout the Cold War.

'Strategic stability' and the appropriate means of assuring such a mutually beneficial outcome are generally associated with two inter-related criteria. Firstly, there is the need to maintain 'arms-race stability' in order not to provide an incentive to build *excessive* nuclear capabilities that would likely lead to a sub-optimal 'arms race'.[27] Such a situation would strengthen each party's perception that the other side had adversarial intentions and reinforce the foundations for the nuclear rivalry itself. Even more dangerous is the potential that one side may temporarily perceive to have a strategic advantage. These 'strategic windows', when combined with competition and insecurity, could lead to pressures for preventive war.[28] Secondly, 'crisis stability' is the need not to provide any incentive for either side to undertake a pre-emptive strike. The side with a first-strike capability would, during any tense crisis situation, be tempted to make use of such an advantage. This could range from a greater willingness to escalate a crisis to scenarios in which disarming and/or decapitating attacks are indeed contemplated. Yet this reality would only increase the anxiety of the opposing side and lead it to prepare pre-emptive-strike plans of its own. Both sides would share 'first-strike anxiety' and be under pressure to reduce negative control over their respective nuclear arsenals and to instigate destabilising postures with higher levels of alert and reductions in the necessary warning signals to initiate a nuclear attack. The possibilities for accidental escalation and brinkmanship, where miscommunication and false intelligence can inadvertently lead to a nuclear exchange, would be dramatically increased.

The need to maintain strategic stability was frequently cited in negative critiques of the American tendency to rely on counter-force 'war-fighting' capabilities during the Cold War. A counter-force strategy would provide denial capabilities that, while rationalised as a feasible means of retaliation, would also be necessary for a disarming first strike.[29] Silo-busting nuclear warheads would be capable of neutralising an adversary's C^3 system and its arsenal of strategic weapons, and any residual retaliation could be blunted and neutralised by a thick area-defence capability. In response to such denial capabilities, an adversary would also likely turn to measures to assure its own retaliatory capabilities. Both crisis- and arms-race-*instability* would thereby be stimulated. There *may* be some strategic benefits to a counter-force approach. As proponents are quick to point out, counter-force capabilities could be used to reinforce the credibility of American deterrence and to provide some damage-limitation capabilities in the event of deterrence failure. Irrespective of the desire to attain a first-strike capability, let alone to undertake a first-strike attack, the counter-force element in American targeting policy does remain far less persuasive when judged in light of these conditions for 'strategic stability'.

Rogue states and military interventionism

The primary rationale for the new triad strategy has been the asymmetrical regional challenge posed by its rogue-state adversaries. These deterrence relationships are antagonistic and, given the imbalance of power between the principal players, potentially unstable. Unlike during the Cold War, the United States does have the capability to intervene militarily against these adversaries. North Korea remains perhaps the most militarily capable of rogue states, in terms of conventional and unconventional capabilities. While its massive conventional military and suspected CB capabilities, and limited nuclear arsenal, would be sufficient to cause enormous damage to American and South Korean forces, and likely to Japan as well, they would still only be able to forestall the inevitable demise of its regime temporarily.

The asymmetrical nature of these relationships represents a significant departure from the context of the Cold War period, and makes traditional arguments against the acquisition of counter-force capabilities more ambiguous. TMD would be useful as a means of assuring American allies, and of preventing any strategic decoupling of American interests from those of its allies owing to a rogue state's regional WMD capabilities and the perceived imbalance in American resolve. Strategic defences would, meanwhile, prevent any future American disengagement from the region. But it remains to be seen whether a more proportionate nuclear response would, in fact, increase the credibility of the American deterrent. It might have some marginal impact against a threat of CB use by a rogue state; a high-yield nuclear response to deter such attacks might not be appropriate, while a conventional response might lack effectiveness. As logical as such a perspective may be, one should not casually dismiss the deterrence value of either a counter-value nuclear response and/or a conventional military campaign that would eliminate the regime of the rogue state foolish enough to attempt such brinkmanship. The risk of such a response might be marginally lower, but the devastating consequences of a wrong decision should encourage caution on the part of any rational actor. Indeed, in the event that a rogue state were sufficiently delusional as to risk such destruction, it remains to be seen whether a more proportionate nuclear response would have any significant impact on the deterrence of such an adversary.

It is true, however, that such weapons might provide a degree of escalation dominance in the midst of a limited military campaign.[30] After all, the credibility of a rogue state's deterrent threat would be greatly magnified in the midst of military conflict, which in turn could have the commensurate effect of limiting American military objectives. A rogue state could even reinforce its intrawar deterrence threat by launching a demonstration attack, with the promise of sequential attacks if the United States did not withdraw. Nuclear counter-force weapons that are capable of destroying a rogue state's strategic WMD capabilities could be used to threaten a disarming retaliatory attack in the event of such coercion, which could, therefore, deter a rogue state from relying on such extreme threats early in any such conflict. The uncertainty of successfully penetrating deployed missile-defence systems could further lessen the attractiveness of such an option. Measures to buttress intrawar deterrence could be especially useful during a limited conflict, though any deterrence value would decline significantly in the light of more ambitious American military objectives (e.g. regime change).

Damage limitation against these adversaries in the event of deterrence failure is both prudent and feasible. Given the American unfamiliarity with the political processes and decision-making procedures of these rogue regimes, and the possibility that the strategic culture of rogue states might not be so amenable to the otherwise persuasive logic of deterrence, the possibility of deterrence failure – even a 'bolt-out-of-the-blue' attack – cannot be discounted.[31] Perhaps more realistically, a US military campaign against such adversaries would still be both possible and seen as a necessity, which would dramatically increase the possible failure of deterrence and, as a consequence, the need for damage limitation. Missile defence could conceivably blunt a modest ballistic-missile attack, while passive defence measures could play a complementary role by minimising the consequences of a CB attack on the US military and any civilians in the vicinity.[32] Damage limitation would be even more complete with the pre-emptive use of bunker-busters and ADWs that would be able to neutralise these capabilities actively prior to their employment. Conventional counter-force weapons would, given the stigma associated with nuclear weapons, be the primary means of pre-emptively disarming an opponent. But even critics of the new triad concede that there may be strategic assets in 'moderately deep and precisely located' HDBTs that only nuclear weapons, and especially EPWs, could neutralise.[33]

Moreover, it remains to be seen whether the American development of these denial capabilities would indeed increase the value of WMD to these rogue states, and, therefore, destabilise arms-race stability in these relationships. It is unlikely – if not impossible – that rogue states would indeed be dissuaded from pursuing such exotic unconventional capabilities, as these do provide a primary defence against any American-led conventional military campaign. But the fact that rogue states view WMD as an asymmetrical counter to American nuclear and conventional power means that any extension of such capabilities would likely have only a contributory effect on WMD proliferation, e.g. an increased incentive for a more robust and survivable WMD deterrent.[34] In other words, a latent arms-race dynamic already exists between the US and its rogue-state adversaries. This is founded on the fundamental imbalance of power between the adversaries, which any new counter-force capabilities inherent in the new triad would be unlikely to increase substantially.

This approach does, however, promise to provide an incentive for either side to strike first during a crisis. The United States might have some increased capability to deter a rogue state from initiating hostilities in the first place. But this advantage must be balanced by the recognition that, by having capabilities tailored to enable military interventions, the US might be equally willing to use military force unilaterally as a means of dealing with rogue-state proliferators. The incentive for 'war initiation', to undertake counter-proliferation campaigns (either reactive or pre-emptive) with potentially ambitious regime-change objectives, could thereby increase. This would be a recipe for inadvertent escalation, as the United States would find itself in intrawar deterrence situations that – given the increased risk of a rogue state actually employing WMD – would increase the pressure for it to undertake disarming strikes using conventional *and* nuclear counter-force capabilities. American plans and capabilities for such strikes, alongside the potential feasibility of a disarming or decapitating strike, would only increase the attractiveness of this option.

Even if the United States did somehow restrain itself from launching a first strike, such a situation inevitably places increased pressure on a rogue state to use its own strategic-deterrent capabilities. The new triad's emphasis on damage limitation and specialised counter-force capabilities would be seen as offering a definite first-strike advantage against a rogue state's more modest unconventional capabilities. The uncertainty of whether American objectives are indeed limited during any counter-proliferation campaign would increase the pressure to escalate the conflict prematurely with WMD use. At the very least, a rogue state would begin to rely on ever-more destabilising employment strategies for its own deterrent, especially if the goal is to provide a degree of positive control during the more complicated situation of intrawar deterrence. A good example is Saddam Hussein's reported pre-delegation of launch authority over Iraq's CB weapons to local commanders to assure retaliation after a decapitating strike on Baghdad during the Gulf War.[35] The temptation to 'launch-under-attack' (LUA) in order to assure retaliation in the event of intrawar deterrence failure or to LOW of an impending first strike would be especially dangerous given their uncertain early-warning and C^3 capabilities.[36] One should also not discount the possible attraction of alternative delivery systems. Cruise missiles are both ideal for a bio-weapon attack and proliferating widely,[37] while prepositioned WMD devices – while certainly a high-risk threat strategy – combine very attractive coercive advantages and immunity to any American counter-force attack.[38]

The knowledge that a rogue-state WMD attack has become potentially more attractive would only increase American incentives to undertake a first strike that would prevent such an occurrence. Even if pressure for a pre-emptive nuclear strike were discounted, perhaps owing to the sense of security provided by sophisticated conventional capabilities and missile-defence systems, this does not mean that such confidence in American non-nuclear capabilities is warranted. Conventional capabilities might not be sufficient to destroy a rogue state's WMD capabilities, while missile defence remains plagued with uncertain and untested technology. Indeed, there is no real surety that new nuclear-counter-force weapons would be capable of completely eliminating a rogue state's WMD arsenal. The end result could simply be the successful use of a rogue state's WMD capabilities and, as a consequence, severe US counter-retaliation (up to and including nuclear weapons).

The new triad strategy may provide the means of dealing with deterrence failure, but on balance it also threatens to create situations that facilitate that very failure. One should not dismiss the benefits that such a strategy could develop, in terms of damage limitation and intrawar deterrence. Yet there are serious costs to such a strategy that must be taken into account. Of course, these costs might be viewed as a necessary evil if, for example, crisis instability and eventual deterrence failure were seen as inevitable outcomes of these asymmetrical relationships. In that case, the new triad would at least provide some capability, uncertain as it might be, to limit the worst excesses of such an occurrence. But if this situation is not as grave as that portrayed, and if latent crisis instability promises to be ameliorated by other means, then the disadvantages of such a strategy would outweigh any such benefits.

Prospects for strategic nuclear stability

An implicit component of the new triad strategy appears to be directed at such major powers as China and Russia, both of which are established nuclear-weapon states that – while not direct adversaries of the United States – have sufficient strategic capabilities to be considered potential near-peer competitors. These relationships are, therefore, marked with a degree of ambiguity that are not found in either US relations with its close allies, such as Canada and the United Kingdom, or with its adversaries, whether they are the rogue states of today or the Soviet 'evil empire' of the Cold War. Yet the new triad's promise of escalation dominance is not limited to current regional adversaries. Indeed, the capabilities envisioned by the new triad imply a dominance over (but not invulnerability to) these potential major powers that would have been previously impossible. This is more of a concern with Russia, as the Chinese arsenal has been sufficiently small since its inception in 1964 as to question its retaliatory survivability against an American (or Russian) first strike. But the reinforcement of this long-standing strategic advantage vis-à-vis China, and its expansion to seek superiority over the much more formidable Russian nuclear arsenal, would constitute an attempt at defining deterrence, not as mutual vulnerability to assured destruction, but rather as unilateral American nuclear superiority.[39]

The Chinese nuclear deterrent is certainly vulnerable to this primacist vision. China has long maintained a 'minimum deterrent' based on a modest second-strike capability (e.g. a 'minimal means of reprisal'). This capability is modest indeed, as it is estimated to only have 18–20 liquid-fuelled DF-5 ballistic missiles with sufficient range to target the continental United States. While China could reinforce this capability by deploying its single *Xia*-class SSBN (armed with 16 JL-1 SLBMs) on patrol near the United States, this submarine has not undertaken a single deterrence patrol since its commission in 1981 and remains stationary at its naval base. More realistically, China does have a capability to deter the United States by targeting its deployed forces and allies in the Pacific. For example, American military assets at Guam are vulnerable to the shorter-range DF-4 ICBM, while US military bases in Japan could be targeted by China's DF-3 medium-range ballistic missile (MRBM). The number of these theatre missiles remains limited, with between 12 and 20 DF-4 ICBMs and up to 16 operational DF-3 MRBMs.[40]

This nuclear arsenal, with its quantitative and qualitative limitations, has always been highly vulnerable to an American first strike, and it does appear that the capabilities inherent in the new triad strategy would only reinforce this advantage. The US ability to locate and destroy these targets would likely increase with the addition of EPWs that could neutralise the cave-based DF-4 (or at least to destroy functional access to these HDBTs), and depressed-trajectory, silo-busting SLBMs that can be more effective against any DF-5 missile silos that are placed on heightened alert. Indeed, the shift of American SLBM forces to the Pacific seems to point towards a renewed interest in such targeting scenarios.[41] Yet such an assessment must be qualified by the recognition that the United States has long maintained a significant first-strike advantage against these forces. Indeed, Chinese defence planners have kept faith in the survivability of their minimum deterrent despite this first-strike threat, which seems to represent the perspective that a splendid first strike *might* simply be too onerous or difficult to prosecute successfully. From such a logic, the American nuclear counter-force advantage remains so large that any improvements will likely only have marginal benefits, and might not be sufficient to negate a Chinese minimum reprisal. A critical factor is, therefore, the possibility that a technologically workable strategic-defence system, in addition to TMD systems in the Pacific, could be capable of intercepting the limited Chinese ICBM/MRBM deterrent.[42] It remains to be seen whether China, if confronted with such a combination of offensive and defensive denial capabilities, would continue to maintain faith in its own retaliatory option.

If a splendid first strike against the Chinese deterrent is potentially feasible, one must then question whether such a situation would be prudent or would benefit American national security. The deterrence value of retaliatory punishment should not be underestimated, especially given the fact that China is considered a relatively risk-adverse state that has neither the more irrational or dangerous attributes commonly associated with rogue states, nor is likely to be invaded by a United States fixated on regime change. However, some benefits might be accrued in the event that the US finds itself on the precipice of a *limited* military conflict with China. This is not in the realm of the impossible, as the Taiwan Strait remains a potential flashpoint in which Chinese resolve to regain de facto sovereignty over Taiwan and American security guarantees to that island state could very well lead to military conflict. Even the NPR notes that 'China is a country that could be involved in an immediate or potential contingency'.[43] In such a situation, the ability to neutralise the Chinese deterrent effectively could – as in the case of rogue states – prevent any form of deterrence by China and provide further escalation dominance in the event that China brandishes its own deterrent or, less probably, risks undertaking a limited nuclear strike. The threat of being able to respond successfully on any escalatory level to China could convince its leaders of American resolve to use force to prevent forcible reunification with Taiwan and, therefore, to deter such a prospect in the first place. Alternatively, in the event that military conflict occurs, the new triad strategy could maximise American conventional superiority and minimise the possibility that the conflict would feature nuclear escalation.[44] If American strategic superiority fails to prevent Chinese nuclear use, the United States would have an ability to mitigate the impact of such deterrence failure.

These advantages are, however, balanced by their less than beneficial impact on strategic stability. On the one hand, there is an increased possibility that the new triad would, when compared to the rogue-state scenario, lead to Sino-US arms-race instability. It is true that the current Chinese strategic-force modernisation, involving MIRV-capable long-range ICBMs (the DF-31 and DF-31A) and a new SSBN with long-range

SLBMs (JL-2), is only tenuously connected to American nuclear-weapon developments. In fact, a more probable explanation is the need to modernise the archaic Chinese nuclear-force structure, as opposed to an arms race 'action–reaction' dynamic generated by the new triad's vision of improved denial capabilities. But one should also not dismiss casually the possibility that this could change. Chinese defence planners have long maintained a limited deterrent in the face of the massive nuclear-counter-force capabilities of the United States and the offensive leg of the new triad appears unlikely to alter this fundamental assessment. But missile-defence systems promise to transform this calculus, since any minimal means of reprisal that survives an American counter-force first strike would be sufficiently small as to be highly (but not totally) vulnerable to interception. If technologically mature missile-defence systems are fielded in the Pacific and the continental United States, it is likely that these fears would fuel arguments for further improvements to offset such an American advantage. Potential quantitative and qualitative changes include 'MIRVed' ballistic missiles, mobile ICBMs and survivable SLBMs, counter-measures and penetration aids, hypersonic ballistic missiles and cruise missiles, and anti-satellite weapons and other defence-suppression capabilities that could neutralise components of any BMD system.[45] These developments might not entail the beginnings of a full-blown arms race, as either country might not have sufficient adversarial intentions to transform prudent force modifications into aggressive arms racing. But the potential of such a negative outcome would be significantly increased.

On the other hand, the very logic of American nuclear superiority – which is most robust when one combines pre-emptive first strikes with active defences – would likely create significant incentives for a first strike during any crisis situation. China might currently maintain a no-first-use pledge, but it would not be impossible that it would feel sufficient pressure to adopt a pre-emptive strike posture in the event of a crisis on such a vital issue as its sovereignty over Taiwan, with the attendant risk in the miscommunication of nuclear signals and increased pressure for American pre-emption. Indeed, American missile-defence capabilities would be based on a number of vulnerable radar and interceptor sites, which offer a whole host of potential 'soft targets' that would be tempting to neutralise early in any serious crisis.[46]

Of course, qualitative and quantitative improvements, alongside various passive defence measures such as hardening or increased road and rail mobility, might improve the survivability of this nuclear arsenal and lessen the need for such first-strike planning. But Chinese nuclear-war planners may be forced to ignore existing concerns over maintaining negative control of their forces and decrease the response time to launch retaliatory strikes, potentially adopting a LOW posture to avoid a disarming or decapitating strike, with all its potential for false warning and accidental nuclear war. Alternatively, China might seek to follow the US lead by developing plans for a limited nuclear strike or nuclear conflict over the Taiwan Strait, which, in fact, would match the growing Chinese emphasis on 'limited deterrence' or the ability to use nuclear weapons to deter conventional attacks and to provide escalation control.[47] Of course, this would entail a robust command-and-control and a LUA capability that might be impossible for China to achieve and, perhaps more importantly, would carry the risk of brinkmanship and inadvertent nuclear use.

The new triad strategy would offer the United States a potential deterrence advantage in the event of military conflict in the Taiwan Strait. Retaliatory punishment might be sufficient for the general deterrence of China, but deterrence-by-denial capabilities would in turn be useful as a means of compensating for an imbalance of resolve in any conflict over Taiwan. This could either reinforce the specific deterrence of Chinese aggression in this instance or provide a degree of intrawar deterrence that keeps the conflict 'limited'. But the costs associated with such a strategy should not be dismissed lightly. It might be premature to consider China's strategic modernisation to be an incipient arms race, but there is an inherent potential for just such a dynamic to gather momentum. Less remarkable would be the pressure to adopt destabilising launch postures, which might appear benign and hypothetically threatening at the moment, but could eventually put American damage-limitation capabilities to the test during any future crisis.

Russia poses a more difficult challenge to the realisation of American nuclear superiority. As the heir to that of the Soviet Union, the Russian deterrent still maintains a massive strategic arsenal consisting of 3,500 deployed strategic warheads, which are expected to decline to the 1,700–2,200 that were agreed in the Moscow Treaty. Its land-based forces, which have traditionally been the backbone of the Russian strategic arsenal, are currently composed of 548 operational ICBMs armed with 2,000 warheads. This consists of 291 single-warhead road-mobile SS-25 ICBMs and 258 silo-based ICBMs, which includes the 'MIRVed' Soviet-era SS-18 and SS-19 alongside the recent addition of the single-warhead SS-27 (*Topol*-M). These ICBMs are joined with a sea-based force of 12 SSBNs, armed with 192 'MIRVed' SLBMs that carry a total of 672 warheads, and 78 *Blackjack* and *Bear* bombers armed with a variety of ALCMs and gravity bombs.[48]

Nuclear superiority requires sufficient counter-force capabilities to destroy the majority of Russian strategic assets in the event of a first strike, and strategic defences that could hypothetically blunt the worst excesses of any Russian residual retaliation and, therefore, significantly reduce (if not eliminate) American societal vulnerability. A splendid first strike was impossible during the latter years of the Cold War, but it does appear that the qualitative improvements to the American arsenal, alongside the continuing deterioration of Russia's, have *potentially* made such a strike feasible. This is the view of Lieber and Press, who have constructed an analytical model of an American first strike on Russian targets and concluded that a disarming first strike is now hypothetically possible.[49] The dilapidated condition of Russia's nuclear arsenal may have blunted its edge, but perhaps more importantly, it has led to a deployment scheme that minimises the number of necessary counter-force targets to be destroyed. After all, Russia's road-mobile ICBMs are located in 40 garrison bases, while its strategic bombers are stationed in two air force bases and its shrinking SSBN fleet is generally stationary in three highly vulnerable ports. The sheer size of the Russian nuclear arsenal means that damage limitation could not be attempted by a missile-defence shield alone, no matter how robust or multi-layered, but such strategic defences could be useful in the event that a battery of SS-25 is away from its garrison or if a SSBN is away from its port on deterrence patrol.

The Lieber and Press model does have certain disadvantages, most clearly in the fact that such a disarming strike would have to be sufficiently quick and unexpected that Russian forces would neither raise their alert status, nor retaliate at the first sign of such an attack.[50] This problem might be lessened by the deterioration of Russia's early-warning network, particularly the deployment problems of satellite constellations and gaps in radar coverage, but it cannot be completely dismissed.[51] As such, it may indeed be premature to discuss the 'end of MAD' or 'nuclear primacy', as the very existence of such a situation is debatable and, given the disastrous consequences of a miscalculation, it remains to be seen whether the United States would ever be willing to test such a proposition in the first place.

Even if such a situation were possible, one can also question whether the United States would be able to obtain any advantages. Nuclear superiority, aside from fulfilling the aim of reducing American societal vulnerability, would likely provide only marginal benefits to the deterrence of Russia. There is little evidence that the US's long-standing deterrence of the Soviet Union, with its more ambitious and deadly nuclear arsenal, was ever insufficient for the task. Nor is there any comparable situation to the Soviet threat against Europe, or even the current challenge posed by triangular deterrence of the US by rogue adversaries. Unlike either rogue states or China, there does not exist a potential flashpoint between the two countries that could lead to military conflict. It is true that if Russia did become a more risk-prone and expansionist state, and if American security guarantees to countries in Eastern Europe and Russia's 'near abroad' were ever tested (in Ukraine for example), then an environment defined by American nuclear superiority could provide some marginal benefits to deterrence or the ability to dominate escalation levels and to place the United States in a strategically advantageous position.[52] But in the current environment, such a vision might be judged more feasible than strategically prudent.

Even more importantly, an American attempt to attain blatant nuclear superiority – irrespective of its meaningful feasibility – would inevitably lead to a Russian effort to reaffirm a situation of mutual vulnerability, and to do so in a far more adversarial context. Russia is already upgrading its nuclear arsenal, and while this is likely driven by the need to modernise and/or to replace ageing nuclear launch vehicles, there is little doubt that some attention is being paid to assuring the country's retaliatory capability. Qualitative improvements include research into developing hypersonic and manoeuvrable warheads for its fifth-generation *Topol* series of ICBMs, which would allow these systems to better evade any workable American strategic defence. Quantitative changes include Russia's intention, with the demise of the START II Treaty in 2002, to maintain a MIRV strategic capability. For example, though both the SS-18 and SS-19 are expected to retire, a modest amount (30–50) of each will have their service life extended and will retain their multiple-warhead arsenals. The SS-27 *Topol*-M might be the new replacement missile and is designed to carry a single warhead, but there are indications that this missile might be modified for multiple 'MIRVed' warheads in 2009, when START I prohibitions on such changes expire.[53]

Russia's strategic arsenal will shrink in the next few years, but with fifth-generation launch vehicles for its land-based forces (the SS-27 and the road-mobile SS-X-27), as well as its sea-based leg (the *Borey*-class SSBN armed with 'MIRVed' *Bulava* missiles), there is the potential for a more subtle qualitative arms-race dynamic to develop between the two nuclear powers. This instability might not create immediate dangers in the currently benign strategic environment. But if relationships do indeed worsen, or if the American drift towards strategic superiority becomes either more evident or explicit, then one could expect more overt off-setting measures to assure the survivability of the Russian deterrent. These could include increased deterrence patrols by its road-mobile ICBMs and SSBN fleet, an expanded use of MIRV technology alongside more survivable and mobile ballistic missiles, reliance on evasive nuclear-launch vehicles such as hypersonic manoeuvrable ballistic missiles and stealthy cruise missiles, and perhaps a reversion to the Soviet Union's suspected exploration of using prepositioned nuclear devices as the ultimate means of survivability.[54] Neither side would seek an arms race, but the perception that would underlie such changes in force structure by either country would likely generate its own momentum for arms-racing behaviour.

An additional means of ensuring the survivability of the Russian arsenal would be renewed reliance on its traditional LOW posture, possibly combined with an increased speed in nuclear-launch authorisation, in order to prevent a fully disarming surprise attack. This posture grew out of the Soviet era's highly centralised nuclear command-and-control system which, as it was particularly vulnerable to an American decapitating strike, emphasised the launching of missiles on receipt of warning of attack. As noted earlier, the LOW posture carries significant dangers of false warnings and accidental escalations during a crisis.[55] This would become specifically acute during a Russian crisis scenario, given the incomplete coverage of Russia's early-warning radar and satellites and the crisis-induced pressure to launch a first-strike salvo of its own.

Crisis instability could be reduced if Russia, rather than relying on a (potentially false) warning of an attack during a crisis, activated its *Perimetr* 'dead hand' launch system, which promises a quasi-automatic retaliation by Russia's strategic ICBM arsenal in the event of confirmed nuclear detonations on Russian territory, e.g. a total disruption in communications, alongside sensor detection of nuclear blasts. This extreme LUA posture would eliminate the potential for the LOW posture to have an error in its early-warning system, and could lessen the incentive for a first strike. But this option does carry its own risks, given its extreme command-and-control centralisation and the possibility of errors generated by sensor and communication disruptions. [56] In any event, the possibility of American nuclear superiority could mean that *Perimetr*, even if activated, might not have any survivable missiles to launch. Russia would likely be forced to rely on the worst of both worlds, meaning a primary reliance on LOW, alongside an increased readiness to undertake a pre-emptive first strike, and its uncertain 'dead hand' LUA launch system used as a back up.[57]

The Russian reaction to the new triad strategy poses the greatest long-term challenge. Not only is nuclear superiority potentially an unattainble or unrealistic goal, especially given the likely Russian reaction to rectify any perceived imbalance, but there are also few, if any, advantages inherent in such a strategic position once it is attained, and plenty of costs that promise to reduce strategic stability between the two countries substantially. The relationship may indeed be sufficiently robust at the moment to dismiss the potential of arms-race or crisis instability, as the adversarial rivalry that would make these two factors more blatantly dangerous is simply not present. But one should discount neither the dangers associated with such instability, nor the long-term potential of escalation towards a more overt adversarial dynamic. The new triad strategy may indeed be a means of 'shaping the new security environment' that foresees potential problems with peer competitors in the future. However, attention must be paid to ensure that any such preparations for a worst-case scenario do not become a self-fulfilling prophecy.

CONCLUSION

The new triad is not a fundamentally revolutionary approach to American nuclear strategy. Many of its components, from the now-abandoned attempt to research nuclear bunker-busters to the initial deployment of GBIs for strategic missile defence, have direct precursors in the Clinton administration. The current administration may, however, be less abashed about promoting these controversial developments, and indeed has placed a particular emphasis on advertising the originality of many of these policies. But the new triad, as it has been envisioned and partially implemented in the last few years, has clear antecedents in American counter-proliferation policy of the 1990s.

Despite this continuity, it is equally true that there is indeed something 'new' in the new triad. While undertaking steps to incorporate conventional capabilities in lieu of nuclear weapons, the Bush administration has also forcefully advocated policies that signify a high-level consensus on and support for the incorporation of counter-proliferation as an integral mission of America's strategic forces. Rogue-state proliferators are no longer viewed as a secondary threat that could be contained through quiet diplomacy and traditional non-proliferation measures. The perception of this threat's ultimate inevitability necessitates a far more robust approach that relies on American strategic capabilities to deny, or at least to mitigate, any asymmetrical advantages from WMDs. American strategic power has been prioritised as the critical means of dealing with the challenge of WMD proliferation.

This position represents a new phase in the evolution of American nuclear strategy. Nuclear deterrence was initially directed against the Soviet Union and predicated on the nuclear superiority of American strategic forces. While ideas of MAD may have captured the public imagination by the 1960s, actual nuclear-weapons policy maintained its focus on attaining some degree of strategic 'advantage' against the Soviet adversary. Disarming counter-force attacks, pre-emptive war-planning and other war-fighting capabilities were consistently incorporated as crucial elements of American nuclear strategy. With Nixon's focus on sufficiency, and Carter and Reagan's emphasis on countervailing and prevailing in a protracted nuclear war, the search to obtain ever-more-lethal war-fighting capabilities was expanded. At this point, doctrine shifted away from the idea of MAD and began to reflect a policy that was born out of the long-standing discomfort with the idea of *mutual* deterrence.

The post-Cold War period witnessed both the demise of an old adversary and growing recognition of the threat posed by WMD-armed regional foes. American nuclear strategy would, however, continue to play a key role in this new strategic threat environment. It would focus on adversaries marked not by strategic parity and potential superiority, but rather by strategic weakness and reliance on asymmetrical means of countering American advantage. American nuclear superiority against these types of adversaries already exists on paper, though this does not mean that US deterrence or dissuasion strategies are effective. Thus, the possibility of asymmetrical means of recreating a situation of de facto mutual deterrence has forced the United States to contemplate reinforcing this superiority by developing capabilities to counter any asymmetrical means of deterrence. This entails what Jason Ellis calls a 'full-spectrum response', including not only more traditional non-proliferation measures, but also a denial strategy to 'defeat, defend against, and operate in the context of NBC [nuclear, biological and chemical] weapons and, if needed, overcome the effects of NBC use'.[1]

This development of counter-force and damage-limiting capabilities designed to facilitate American military interventionism is certainly far more ambitious than the traditional 'deterrence' strategy of nuclear weapons during the Cold War. But an implicit emphasis of the deliberate new triad strategy appears, equally, to be tailored against such potential rivals as Russia and China. Indeed, such is the nature of capability-based planning, whereby the acquisition of capabilities for one contingency can be understood to have a utility for or an impact on others. Whether the new triad is indeed *intentionally* directed at potential near-peer competitors remains the subject of conjecture. This outcome may have less to do with the external threat environment and more to do with internal bureaucratic inertia, debate or technological momentum. That being said, one should not underestimate America's long-standing desire to reduce its societal vulnerability to a nuclear attack and, thereby, to escape the seductive (or horrific) logic of MAD. Nor should one ignore the growing American consensus on a primacist grand strategy, which this administration – far more than any of its predecessors – appears to have embraced.

Motivations aside, the new triad strategy as currently envisioned poses definite dilemmas and complications for strategic stability. Rogue states are the most explicit rationale for the new triad and represent the strongest case for the development of counter-force capabilities. The United States currently faces a situation in which its superpower role demands the capability to intervene in regional conflicts or to invade rogue regimes that pose an imminent threat in a cost-effective way. Military conflicts with regional adversaries armed with WMD are, despite the current imbroglio in Iraq, a possibility in the future. It would, therefore, be strategically prudent to develop both conventional and nuclear counter-force capabilities that would facilitate such interventionism and bolster deterrence and dissuasion strategies, even if this means preparation for the possibility of deterrence failure. Even if a rogue state reacts to such a development with an increased reliance on WMD, the strategic threat environment facing the United States would still necessitate such a posture. To do otherwise, given the possibility of military conflict, would simply not be in the US national interest. Fortunately, the asymmetrical nature of these adversarial relationships reduces the possibility of this type of arms-racing behaviour, as many potential adversaries can ill afford and would find it difficult to acquire effective WMD forces.

The potential for crisis instability, which increases the chances of military conflict and WMD use by either a rogue state or the United States, is a spectre that casts its shadow over the new triad and represents a more valid reason to be cautious with this strategy. Prudent planning for an eventuality such as deterrence failure might not be so sensible if it transforms this eventuality into a certainty. This, however, must also be balanced against the inevitable paradox of a deterrence or dissuasion strategy: that the more credible (and usable/tailored) US nuclear forces become, the less likely that such weapons would be used, unless adversaries are undeterrable and the US remains intent on following through with its interventionist agenda. Thus, a critical issue that must be assessed is the extent to which crisis instability, rather than being a direct consequence of the new triad strategy, is inherent in these adversarial relationships themselves. Crisis instability may simply be an inevitable result of an asymmetrical adversarial relationship. While the new triad strategy could potentially contribute to such destabilisation, and would not be an optimal solution to the problem, it might still be considered a problematic necessity against these types of adversaries.[2] In other words, while stability may be an important goal in these kinds of relationships, it is certainly not the only yardstick by which this strategy should be judged. The requirement to 'roll back' WMD proliferation could be seen as a goal that justifiably trumps strategic stability, especially if the US attains the ability to control escalation successfully and to neutralise an adversary's WMD capability.

The military necessity of planning for intrawar deterrence and deterrence failure against rogue states must also be balanced against wider strategic considerations. Foremost among these is the potential that the new triad, while useful against these weak adversaries, poses more significant problems for strategic nuclear stability among more important actors. Nuclear superiority is certainly a feasible proposition with China (and may have been the case since China became a nuclear-weapon state). In this case, however, the costs associated with strategic instability – including a greatly increased potential for geostrategic competition and the likelihood of transforming an ambiguous relationship into an adversarial one – should instil caution in even the most hawkish advocates of superiority. A similar reasoning can also be applied to Russia, though in this case one can more easily question the feasibility of and benefits associated with nuclear superiority, and the potential catastrophic consequences of strategic instability between two heavily armed nuclear powers. Nuclear superiority may entail a more favourable position in the event that an adversarial relationship develops with either country. But given the currently benign threat environment, and the likelihood that such a policy would indeed inject a preventable adversarial dynamic into either relationship, such a strategy would ultimately be self defeating.

This study has focused on the new triad's consequences for strategic stability. It is possible that some strategic advantage, in the event of intrawar deterrence and deterrence failure, can be gained against rogue-state adversaries. However, this strategy also promises simultaneously to increase first-strike anxiety on the part of the rogue state and the incentive for war initiation and destabilising launch postures among these fragile adversarial relationships. This disadvantage *could* be rationalised as a 'lesser of two evils', in the event that deterrence failure and damage limitation are seen as sufficiently pressing and inevitable. Yet it is much more difficult to rationalise and support a primacist strategy that has the potential to inject a more adversarial element into the nuanced American strategic relationships with China and Russia. This may not be the *intent* of either the NPR or the subsequent policy documents, but the end result of such an approach may be equally as damaging.

It is, however, possible that a more limited variant of the new triad strategy can be developed to minimise its consequences, which is certain to be more practicable in the near term, politically and technologically. This would be heavily dependent on whether nuclear-offensive and missile-defensive counter-force capabilities designed against rogue states, which have some degree of utility, can be disentangled from both a first-strike posture, which stimulates reciprocal fears of pre-emptive or surprise attacks, and the ambitious strategic primacy that is directed at potential major-power adversaries. While this cannot be fully addressed here, there are reasons to be optimistic. A first-strike posture not only requires weapons capable of destroying an adversary's own capabilities, but must be especially designed for prompt and, ideally, stealthy attacks. Moreover, the imbalance of strategic capability between rogue states and potential major-power adversaries points to another means of differentiation. The counter-force requirements against rogue states are far less onerous, and would only require a much more limited capability, than that required for nuclear primacy against either Russia or China.

From this perspective, the primary offensive means of dealing with HDBTs and CB facilities among rogue states should be with small numbers of tactical, air-launched conventional EPWs and ADWs. These weapons would provide the principal means of disarming and defeating a rogue state during military conflict, and compared to strategic or forward-based tactical nuclear weapons, would have clear advantages in terms of their usability for both counter-proliferation and pre-emption. TMDs would provide a complementary damage-limitation capability against the immediate WMD threat posed by rogue states, and would be more technologically feasible than an area-defence system for the continental United States (though coverage would have to be sufficiently wide to protect regional allies against triangular deterrence). Equally as important, theatre defences would not threaten Russia's strategic deterrent and could be sufficiently limited so as not to threaten China's own theatre ballistic-missile force. Strategic missile defence could be developed, but the immediacy of its deployment should decrease and its future architecture should be both limited and clearly delineated.[3]

These conventional capabilities could be supplemented with a limited number of tailored, tactical nuclear-counter-force weapons. These weapons could be used primarily for the more difficult task of intrawar deterrence, where the goal would be to hold key targets hostage in order to deny a rogue state any coercive advantage during a conflict, and as a means of retaliation in the event of WMD use. Accuracy would likely be the most important characteristic, though modest earth-penetration and low-yield capabilities might offer some marginal improvements in destroying certain targets and deterrence value, by lowering any perceptions of self-deterrence.[4] Effort can be made to differentiate this posture from a pre-emptive first-strike posture in order to minimise, if not to eliminate, crisis instability.[5] For example, these warheads could be combined with tactical aircraft, strategic bombers and even ICBMs, as opposed to SLBMs that have advantages in speed and surprise. Such weapons could be based away from airfields that could threaten China and Russia, while transparency or other confidence-building measures could also be adopted if tensions were indeed observed. The requirement for a prompt global-strike capability, evident in CONPLAN-8066, should also be limited to these tactical counter-force weapons and decoupled from strategic nuclear-war planning against either Russia or China. Furthermore, these counter-force weapons could be placed on low alert levels that could be reversed during either a serious crisis scenario or a conflict, at which point greater concern would likely be generated by the possibility of deterrence failure and requirements for damage limitation rather than crisis instability.

This 'limited counter-force capability' could also be differentiated from a more general arsenal of high-yield but less accurate weapons that would be designed for retaliation against both Russia and China. Life-extension programmes should continue with American nuclear-legacy systems, but the need to improve accuracy and ground-burst capability – in quantities that cannot be justified against the rogue-state threat – should be eliminated. This should be combined with efforts to reduce the size of the US–Russian nuclear arsenals substantially, as a counter-value posture would also have much more limited targeting requirements, alongside reductions in launch readiness that would reduce the possibility of accidental or inadvertent nuclear attack. However, care must be taken to ensure that US force reductions are synchronised with those of Russia (in order to minimise any 'windows of opportunity') and are not sufficiently deep as to risk entanglement with the proposed smaller stockpile of accurate, tactical counter-force nuclear weapons. Indeed, simultaneous efforts should also be made to encourage Chinese nuclear modernisation that would both minimise strategic instability and better assure the Chinese arsenal's survivability against any limited American counter-force capability.

This approach has the potential benefit of combining the advantages of the new triad strategy and minimising concerns over such a capability – whether it is justified or not – on the part of Russia and China. Indeed, such a capability would likely be more palatable to European and other allied countries and, as such, minimise any negative impact on the non-proliferation regime that has so worried arms-control and disarmament advocates. This requires a nuanced approach to make sure that limited counter-force capabilities do not create 'unnecessary' damage to more traditional, multilateral approaches to proliferation. On some levels, a limited counter-force approach would certainly cause a certain degree of opprobrium. After all, the nuclear targeting of non-nuclear rogue states clearly raises questions as to a possible American violation of its own 'negative security assurances' that were made as part of the non-proliferation regime, whereby the nuclear powers would not target non-nuclear states with nuclear weapons.[6] That being said, an attempt to minimise, if not to eliminate, the potential negative externalities of a limited counter-force approach could be made. For example, counter-force capabilities might be useful against rogue states, but this does not entail a free rein to research and test low-yield bunker-busters when the current arsenal already has substantial variation in yield size. New nuclear missions could be balanced with a fundamental reassessment of deterrence requirements vis-à-vis Russia, potentially resulting in substantial and verified reductions.

This proposed posture might not be perfect, and further research into potential trade-offs is certainly required. However, it is clear that the existing new triad strategy does deserve a thorough reassessment. Its combination of ambition and hubris may produce useful benefits in American relations with regional adversaries. But if US nuclear strategy appears tailored towards obtaining a first-strike counter-force capability against potential major-power adversaries, it is likely that any benefits would be overshadowed by long-term instability in a number of key strategic nuclear relationships. Unfortunately, the United States seems to some to be enthralled by the potential for indefinite strategic primacy and, at least in some quarters, keen to implement a maximalist new triad strategy. Indeed, components of the new triad have been simmering in the Pentagon for many years and are the *cause célèbre* for a new generation of nuclear-weapon scientists. A bi-partisan consensus has even emerged on the perils of WMD proliferation and the need for US strategic primacy. Currently it appears unlikely that the new triad, despite its continued moderation by an activist Congress that remains keenly aware of its potential for unintended and destabilising consequences, will shift significantly from its primacist foundations.

NOTES

Introduction

1 See *Nuclear Posture Review [Excerpts]* (Washington DC: Department of Defense (DoD), 8 January 2002). The DoD would only release a three-page foreword and a set of slides relating to the NPR. The classified document was, however, leaked to the *Los Angeles Times* and the *New York Times*, which published a number of articles on the document. See Paul Richter, 'US Works Up Plan for Using Nuclear Arms', *Los Angeles Times*, 9 March 2002; William Arkin, 'Secret Plan Outlines the Unthinkable', *Los Angeles Times*, 10 March 2002; John H. Cushman, Jr, 'Rattling New Sabers', *New York Times*, 10 March 2002; Michael R. Gordon, 'US Nuclear Plan Sees New Weapons and New Targets', *New York Times*, 10 March 2002. This paper uses as reference the NPR excerpts that have been posted on John Pike's Globalsecurity.org website: http://www.globalsecurity.org/wmd/library/policy/dod/npr.htm.

2 See Hans M. Kristensen and Joshua Handler, 'The USA and Counter-Proliferation: A New and Dubious Role for US Nuclear Weapons', *Security Dialogue*, vol. 27, no. 4, 1996, pp. 387–99.

3 See Dean Wilkening, *Ballistic-Missile Defence and Strategic Stability*, Adelphi Paper 334 (Oxford: Oxford University Press for the IISS, 2000).

4 Robert Jervis, *The Illogic of American Nuclear Strategy* (Ithaca, NY: Cornell University Press, 1984), p. 75.

5 For a concise articulation on the reasons for this apprehension, see Keith B. Payne, 'Nuclear Deterrence for a New Century', *The Journal of International Security Affairs*, no. 10, Spring 2006, pp. 49–55. For a more in-depth study, see Payne, *Deterrence in the Second Nuclear Age* (Lexington, KY: The University Press of Kentucky, 1996).

6 For more on the difference between coercive and controlling strategies, and the place of deterrence along this continuum, see Lawrence Freedman, *Deterrence* (Cambridge: Polity Press, 2004). For an earlier examination, see Freedman, 'Strategic Coercion', in Freedman, ed., *Strategic Coercion: Concepts and Cases* (Oxford: Oxford University Press, 1998), pp. 15–36.

7 For more on the 'golden age', see Richard Betts, 'A Nuclear Golden Age? The Balance Before Parity', *International Security*, vol. 11, no. 3, Winter 1986–87, pp. 3–33.

Chapter One

1 An earlier version of this chapter was published as McDonough, 'Nuclear Superiority or Mutually Assured Deterrence: The Development of the US Nuclear Deterrent', *International Journal*, vol. 60, no. 3, Summer 2005, pp. 811–23.

2 For more on the argument for the tactical use of nuclear weapons during the Second World War, see Barton J. Bernstein, 'Eclipsed by Hiroshima and Nagasaki: Early Thinking about Tactical Nuclear Weapons', *International Security*, vol. 15, no. 4, Spring 1991, pp. 149–73. An excellent account of the linkage between strategic bombardment and nuclear weapons can be found in Freedman, *The Evolution of Nuclear Strategy*, 3rd edn (Basingstoke: Palgrave Macmillan, 2003), esp. chs 3–4.

3 For more on the nuclear taboo, see Nina Tannenwald, 'The Nuclear Taboo: The United States and the Normative Basis of Nuclear Non-Use', *International Organization*, vol. 53, no. 3, Summer 1999, pp. 433–68 and 'Stigmatizing the Bomb: Origins of the Nuclear Taboo', *International Security*, vol. 29, no. 4, Spring 2005, pp. 5–49.

4 Cited in Scott D. Sagan, *Moving Targets: Nuclear Strategy and National Security* (Princeton, NJ: Princeton University Press, 1989), p. 14.

5 David Alan Rosenberg, 'The Origins of Overkill: Nuclear Weapons and American Strategy, 1945–1960', *International Security*, vol. 7, no. 4, Spring 1983, p. 14.

6 This comment refers to the 1949 *Dropshot* plan, which was the most systematic of these early nuclear-war plans. Other plans included: the *Broiler*, *Bushwacker* and *Half-moon* plans of 1947–48, which emphasised hitting industrial facilities, economic infrastructure and other 'retardation' targets; and the 1949 *Trojan* plan, which added 'withhold' options against certain key cities. See Desmond Ball, *Targeting for Strategic Deterrence*, Adelphi Paper 185 (London: International Institute for Strategic Studies, 1983), ch. 1.

7 Betts, *Nuclear Blackmail and Nuclear Balance* (Washington DC: Brookings, 1987), ch. 2. The Korean War saw ambiguous remarks by Truman during a press conference, in which he stated that 'every weapon' was under consideration for the conflict. The Berlin crisis saw the movement of 60 B-29 bombers, famous for their role in Hiroshima and Nagasaki, to Britain – a signal that can be considered the 'shadow of deterrence'. In addition, the Strategic Air Command was placed on initial alert and, in December 1948, a war plan was approved that called for atomic attacks on 70 Soviet cities, with casualties estimated at 6.7m. See Sagan, *Moving Targets*, ch. 1.

8 Cited in Sagan, *Moving Targets*, p. 16. The National Military Establishment was the precursor organisation to the DoD, which combined the previously separate Department of War and Department of Navy. It was created by the National Security Act of 1947, and would be renamed the DoD in 1949.

9 See Rosenberg, 'The Origins of Overkill', pp. 3–71.

10 See Robert S. Norris, 'Where They Were', *The Bulletin of the Atomic Scientists*, vol. 55, no. 6, November/December 1999, pp. 26–35. Much of this article's evidence comes from the declassified 'History of the Custody and Deployment of Nuclear Weapons: July 1945 Through September 1977', which is a historical narrative that documents the growth of the US nuclear arsenal and the global deployment of nuclear weapons.

11 NSC-68, *United States Objectives and Programs for National Security* (Washington DC: The White House, 7 April 1950), Section 8: http://www.fas.org/irp/offdocs/nsc-hst/nsc-68.htm.

12 Marc Trachtenberg, 'A "Wasting Asset": American Strategy and the Shifting Nuclear Balance, 1949–1954', *International Security*, vol. 13, no. 3, Winter 1988/89, p. 6. For more on preventive-war thinking during this period, see Gian P. Gentile,

'Planning for Preventive War, 1945–1950', *Joint Forces Quarterly*, no. 24, Spring 2000, pp. 68–74.

[13] Cited in Trachtenberg, 'The Bush Strategy in Historic Perspective', in James L. Wirtz and Jeffrey A. Larsen, eds, *Nuclear Transformation: The New US Nuclear Doctrine* (Basingstoke: Palgrave Macmillan, 2005), p. 13. A number of military officers would continue to express sympathy for preventive war after NSC-68 had effectively rejected it, including General George Kenney, Curtis Lemay, Thomas Power, Nathan Twining, Thomas White and Hoyt Vandenberg. See Sagan, 'The Perils of Proliferation: Organization Theory, Deterrence Theory, and the Spread of Nuclear Weapons', *International Security*, vol. 18, no. 4, Spring 1994, pp. 78–9.

[14] For more on the 'new look', see John Lewis Gaddis, *Strategies of Containment: A Critical Appraisal of Postwar American National Security Policy* (Oxford: Oxford University Press, 1982), ch. 5 and Saki Dockrill, *Eisenhower's New-Look National Security Policy, 1953–61* (New York: St Martin's Press, 1996).

[15] Cited in Freedman, *The Evolution of Nuclear Strategy*, p. 78.

[16] *Ibid.*, p. 119.

[17] Cited in Rosenberg, 'The Origins of Overkill', p. 33.

[18] See Gordon H. Chang, 'To the Nuclear Brink: Eisenhower, Dulles, and the Quemoy–Matsu Crisis', *International Security*, vol. 12, no. 4, Spring 1988, pp. 96–123. The six cases of nuclear blackmail are (1) the Korean War; (2) French Indochina in 1954; (3) Matsu and Quemoy in 1954–55; (4) Suez in 1956; (5) Lebanon in 1958; and (6) Matsu and Quemoy in 1958. See Betts, *Nuclear Blackmail and Nuclear Balance*, ch. 2.

[19] Owing to the lack of adequate air-defence systems, the US remained highly vulnerable to Soviet bomber attacks. This vulnerability was only increased by the Soviet thermonuclear capability. A February 1953 research group calculated that a Soviet attack on 100 urban areas with 100 bombs (of which 11 were thermonuclear with a one-megatonne yield) would lead to 19m fatalities. Betts, 'A Nuclear Golden Age?', pp. 12.

[20] Rosenberg, 'The Origins of Overkill', p. 66.

[21] Definitions of tactical nuclear weapons have often rested on the characteristics of the weapon, whether it be range, yield, target, national ownership, delivery vehicle or capability. A better definition would be based on the role of the weapon, whereby strategic use would be based on their independent impact against the enemy and tactical use would be in support of conventional operations. For more on tactical nuclear weapons, see Alistair Millar and Brian Alexander, *Uncovered Nukes: Arms Control and the Challenge of Tactical Nuclear Weapons*, Policy Brief (Washington DC: Fourth Freedom Forum, 30 November 2001).

[22] For more on the formation of SIOP-62, see Rosenberg, 'The Origins of Overkill', pp. 3–71 and Ball, 'The Development of SIOP, 1960–1983', in Ball and Jeffrey Richelson, eds, *Strategic Nuclear Targeting* (Ithaca, NY: Cornell University Press, 1986), pp. 57–83.

[23] Rosenberg, 'The Origins of Overkill', p. 63.

[24] Freedman, *Kennedy's Wars: Berlin, Cuba, Laos, and Vietnam* (Oxford: Oxford University Press, 2000), pp. 94–5. With this plan in mind, the United States called for the creation of 32 fully manned, combat-ready divisions on NATO's central region, of which the US portion would be increased to six divisions.

[25] Cited in Sagan, *Moving Targets*, pp. 26, 28.

[26] Ball, 'Development of the SIOP', p. 66. For a more critical examination of US first-strike capability, see Betts, 'A Nuclear Golden Age?', pp. 3–33.

[27] See Francis J. Gavin, 'The Myth of Flexible Response: American Strategy in Europe during the 1960s', *International History Review*, vol. 23, December 2001, pp. 847–75.

28 Cited in Ball, 'Development of the SIOP', p. 65.

29 Freedman, *The Evolution of Nuclear Strategy*, p. 230. The 1961 Berlin crisis seems to have played a pivotal role in the policy of strengthening nuclear-counter-force capabilities. The USAF advocated a nuclear first-strike during the 1961 crisis in order to limit damage to the United States, while civilian staff planner under Assistant Secretary of Defense Paul H. Nitze developed a secret Berlin-related contingency plan involving a first-strike counter-force attack. See Betts, 'A Golden Age?', p. 18 and Fred Kaplan, 'JFK's First-Strike Plan', *Atlantic Monthly*, vol. 288, no. 3, October 2001, pp. 81–6.

30 Ball, 'Development of the SIOP', p. 70.

31 William Burr and Richelson, 'Whether to "Strangle the Baby in the Cradle": The United States and the Chinese Nuclear Program', *International Security*, vol. 25, no. 3, Winter 2000/01, p. 67.

32 Cited in Terry Terriff, *The Nixon Administration and the Making of US Nuclear Strategy* (Ithaca, NY: Cornell University Press, 1995), p. 22.

33 Richard Smoke, *National Security and the Nuclear Dilemma: An Introduction to the American Experience in the Cold War*, 3rd edn (New York: McGraw-Hill, 1993), ch. 10.

34 Burr, 'The Nixon Administration, the "Horror Strategy", and the Search for Limited Nuclear Options, 1969–1972: A Prelude to the Schlesinger Doctrine', *Journal of Cold War Studies*, vol. 7, no. 3, Summer 2005, p. 54. The concept of sufficiency was, however, still a highly ambiguous one, insofar as it did not fully elaborate on what was sufficient. Any policy could, therefore, be justified. As then-Deputy Secretary of Defense David Packard remarked on the meaning of sufficiency: 'It means that it's a good word to use in a speech. Beyond that it doesn't mean a God-damned thing.' Freedman, *The Evolution of Nuclear Strategy*, p. 325.

35 The triad concept may be associated with Laird, but it does appear to be a concept that has been retroactively applied to previous policies and used as a means to justify the parochial interests underlying those policies. As Freedman notes, the triad appears to have been 'derived less from intellectual compulsion than political convenience', particularly 'the acceptance by the civilian leadership of the pre-existent division of responsibities between the Services'. Freedman, *The Evolution of Nuclear Strategy*, p. 326.

36 Cited in Burr, 'The Nixon Administration', p. 48.

37 Press conference of Schlesinger at the National Press Club, Washington DC, cited in Terriff, *The Nixon Administration*, p. 1.

38 For more on a winnable 'nuclear war', see Colin S. Gray, 'Nuclear Strategy: The Case for a Theory of Victory', *International Security*, vol. 4, no. 1, Summer 1979, pp. 54–87 and Gray and Payne, 'Victory is Possble', *Foreign Policy*, no. 39, Summer 1980, pp. 14–27. For arguments critical of this perspective, see Charles-Philippe David, *Debating Counterforce: A Conventional Approach in a Nuclear Age* (Boulder, CO: Westview Press, 1987) and Jervis, *The Illogic of American Nuclear Strategy*, esp. ch. 3.

39 This scenario was originally detailed in Paul H. Nitze, 'Assuring Strategic Stability in an Era of Détente', *Foreign Affairs*, vol. 54, no. 2, January 1976, pp. 207–32. Also see Gray, 'The Strategic Forces Triad: End of the Road?', *Foreign Affairs*, vol. 56, no. 4, July 1978, pp. 771–89. For a concise critique of this type of vulnerability, see John D. Steinbruner, 'Launch under Attack', *Scientific American*, January 1984, pp. 37–47.

40 Walter Slocombe, 'The Countervailing Strategy', *International Security*, vol. 5, no. 4, Spring 1981, p. 21. For an insightful examination of the development of this strategy, see Warner R. Schilling, 'US Strategic Nuclear Concepts in the 1970s: The Search for Sufficiently Equivalent Countervailing Parity', *International Security*, vol. 6, no. 2, Fall 1981, pp. 48–79.

41 Freedman, *The Evolution of Nuclear Strategy*, p. 387.

42 Jervis, *The Illogic of American Nuclear Strategy*, p. 130. Escalation dominance has its intellectual roots in the work of Herman Kahn at RAND in the 1950s, specifically his idea of the escalation ladder and the need to control and dominate the escalation process.

43 Ball and Robert C. Toth, 'Revising the SIOP: Taking War-Fighting to Dangerous Extremes', *International Security*, vol. 14, no. 4, Spring 1980, p. 68. For more on Reagan's prevailing strategy, see Sagan, *Moving Targets* and Freedman, *The Evolution of Nuclear Strategy*, ch. 26.

44 As pointed out by Jervis, while public pronouncements have changed dramatically, changes to actual targeting and SIOPs have been 'evolutionary'. Jervis, *The Illogic of American Nuclear Strategy*, p. 65.

45 Terriff, *The Nixon Administration*, p. 3.

46 Jervis, *The Illogic of American Nuclear Strategy*, p. 72. For more on the ethnic-targeting controversy, see David T. Cattell and George H. Quester, 'Ethnic Targeting: Some Bad Ideas', in Ball and Richelson, eds, *Strategic Nuclear Targeting* (Ithaca, NY: Cornell University Press, 1986), pp. 267–84.

47 Ball and Toth, 'Revising the SIOP', p. 68. For a good look at the threat of decapitation, see Steinbruner, 'Launch Under Attack', pp. 37–47 and 'Nuclear Decapitation', *Foreign Policy*, no. 45, Winter 1981–82, pp. 18–28.

48 Other weapon concepts included shallow and rigid earth-penetrator weapons; manoeuvrable re-entry vehicles, which would be able to evade Soviet interceptor missiles, to slow down to minimise the impact and to position the warhead for maximum penetration; larger nuclear-weapon yields (up to 22 megatonnes); and rapid retargetable *Minuteman* ICBMs. For more on these concepts, see Ball and Toth, 'Revising the SIOP', pp. 65–92.

49 *Ibid.*, p. 66.

50 See Walter J. Boyne, 'The Rise of Air Defense', *Air Force Magazine*, vol. 22, no. 12, December 1999. The United States, in cooperation with Canada, developed the Pinetree Line and the Distant Early Warning Line in the Arctic. These radar networks were complemented with the Mid-Canada Line, which was initiated by Canada and built entirely with its own resources.

51 Brennan, 'The Case for Missile Defense', *Foreign Affairs*, vol. 47, no. 3, April 1969, p. 433. Of course, it should be noted that the Johnson administration was not the first to examine the feasibility of missile defence. BMD dates back to the 1956 *Nike–Zeus* ABM system pioneered by the US Arny. The *Nike–Zeus* ABM system was finally shelved in 1962, but its successor, the *Nike*-X, would go on to form the core of the Johnson administration's *Sentinel* ABM system.

52 Reagan, 'Address to the Nation on National Security', 23 March 1983, http://www.fas.org/spp/starwars/offdocs/rrspch.htm.

53 For more on the various programmes of the SDI, see Sidney D. Drell, Philip J. Farley and David Holloway, 'Preserving the ABM Treaty: A Critique of the Reagan Strategic Defense Initiative', *International Security*, vol. 9, no. 2, Fall 1984, pp. 51–91 and John A. Jungerman, *The Strategic Defense Initiative: A Critique and a Primer*, Policy Paper 8 (San Diego, CA: Institute on Global Conflict and Cooperation, University of California, 1988).

54 Studies by the Strategic Defense Initiative Organization and the Defense Nuclear Agency cited in Ball and Toth, 'Revising the SIOP', pp. 81–2.

55 Reagan, 'Address to the Nation on National Security'.

56 See Douglas A. Ross, *Coping with Star Wars: Issues for Canada and the Alliance*, Aurora Papers 2 (Ottawa, ON: Canadian Centre for Arms Control and Disarmament, 1985).

Chapter Two

1 Cited in Michael Klare, *Rogue States and Nuclear Outlaws: America's Search for a New Foreign Policy* (New York: Hill and Wang, 1995), p. 4.

2 Andreani, 'The Disarray of US Non-Proliferation Policy', *Survival*, vol. 41, no. 4, Winter 1999–2000, p. 43.

3 See Jason Ellis, 'The Best Defense: Counterproliferation and US National Security', *The Washington Quarterly*, vol. 26, no. 2, Spring 2003, pp. 115–33.

4 See NSPD-17, *National Strategy to Combat Weapons of Mass Destruction* (Washington DC: The White House, December 2002): http://www.fas.org/irp/offdocs/nspd/nspd-17.html. This refers to the unclassified version of the NSPD-17. According to *The Washington Times*, the classified NSPD-17 explicitly allows for nuclear retaliation in the event of a CB attack. See Nicholas Kralev, 'Bush Signs Paper Allowing Nuclear Response', *The Washington Times*, 31 January 2003, A1.

5 Betts, 'The Osirak Fallacy', *The National Interest*, vol. 83, Spring 2006, pp. 25.

6 R.B. Byers, 'The perils of superpower diplomacy: détente, defence and arms control', *International Journal*, vol. 35, no. 3, Summer 1980, p. 521.

7 See Anthony Lake, 'Confronting Backlash States', *Foreign Affairs*, vol. 73, no. 2, March–April 1994, pp. 45–56.

8 See Francis J. Gavin, 'Blasts from the Past: Proliferation Lessons from the 1960s', *International Security*, vol. 29, no. 3, Winter 2004/2005, pp. 100–135. For more on the pre-emptive debate, see Burr and Richelson, 'Whether to "Strangle the Baby in the Cradle"', pp. 54–99.

9 See Dan Stober, 'No experience necessary', *Bulletin of the Atomic Scientists*, vol. 59, no. 2, March/April 2003, pp. 56–63.

10 See Avner Cohen and Burr, 'Israel crosses the threshold', *Bulletin of the Atomic Scientists*, vol. 62, no. 3, May/June 2006, pp. 22–30.

11 The Israeli acquisition of nuclear weapons did not lead to an immediate cascade of nuclear proliferation. Yet it did substantially contribute to the slow and gradual cascade of WMD proliferation – nuclear, biological and chemical – in the Middle East that has since come to define this regional strategic environment. The same delayed proliferation cascade also took place in Asia, as it would only be 30 years until India and Pakistan followed China's example and become declared nuclear powers. Indeed, much of the dangers of the *N*th country problem of the 1950s and 1960s were held in abeyance throughout the Cold War, but would emerge with a vengeance in the post-Cold War period.

12 Commission on Integrated Long-Term Strategy, *Discriminate Deterrence* (Washington DC: US Government Printing Office, 1988), p. 9.

13 Cited in Byers, 'The perils of superpower diplomacy', p. 527. For more on the Carter Doctrine, see Robert H. Johnson, 'The Persian Gulf in US Strategy: A Skeptical View', *International Security*, vol. 14, no. 1, Summer 1989, pp. 123–4.

14 This perspective was reinforced by the ongoing events of the Iran–Iraq War, which featured the massive military mobilisation (including the acquisition and employment of chemical weapons) by two Persian Gulf countries. It was also raised in the Limited Contingency Study by then-Deputy Assistant Secretary of Defense for Regional Programs Paul Wolfowitz during the Carter administration, which noted the possible military threat of Iraq to Kuwait and Saudi Arabia and examined the scenario of an Iraqi invasion against either of these countries. For more on the Wolfowitz study, see Michael Mann, *Rise of the Vulcans: The History of Bush's War Cabinet* (New York: Penguin Books, 2004), ch. 5.

15 See Robert Litwak, *Rogue States and US Foreign Policy: Containment after the Cold War* (Washington DC : Woodrow Wilson Center Press, 2000), ch. 1.

16 *Ibid.*, p. 53.

17 See Klare, *Rogue States and Nuclear Outlaws*, ch. 1.

18 *Ibid.*, p. 26.

19 Patrick E. Tyler, 'US Strategy Plan Calls for Insuring No Rivals Develop: A One-Superpower World', *New York Times*, 7 March 1992. See also Robert Gellman, 'Keeping the US First: the Pentagon would Preclude a Rival Superpower', *Washington Post*, 11 March 1992.

20 The original DPG was reportedly authored by Zalmay Khalilzad under the guidance of then-Secretary of Defense Dick Cheney and Undersecretary of Defense for Policy Wolfowitz. The redrafted DPG guidance was reportedly done by I. 'Scooter' Libby, under the guidance of Cheney. This document was actually seen as being more ambitious than the controversial leaked document, though its vague language and more diplomatic tone lessened any controversy over its release. See Mann, *Rise of the Vulcans*, ch. 13. The Clinton administration appears to have continued with this primacist strategy. See Barry R. Posen and Andrew L. Ross, 'Competing Visions for US Grand Strategy', *International Security*, vol. 21, no. 3, Winter 1996/1997, pp. 5–53.

21 For a history of non-proliferation, see Henry D. Sokolski, *Best of Intentions: America's Campaign Against Strategic Weapons Proliferation* (Westport, CT: Praeger, 2001).

22 One could also add the signing of the Chemical Weapons Convention in 1997, which, along with the NPT and the Biological and Toxic Weapons Convention, would form the three pillars of the WMD-non-proliferation regime. Movement on a Comprehensive Test Ban Treaty and a Fissile Material Cutoff Treaty were also integral to the development of the non-proliferation regime in the 1990s.

23 During the Gulf War, the US mounted 970 air strikes against WMD targets and 1,500 air strikes against Iraqi ballistic-missile capabilities. See Barry R. Schneider, *Future War and Counterproliferation: US Military Responses to NBC Proliferation Threats* (Westport, CT: Praeger, 1999), ch. 7.

24 The danger posed by biological weapons was also reinforced in 1992 by Ken Alibek's defection and subsequent revelations on the true scale of the Soviet Union's biological weapons programme. Alibek had served in various senior capacities in the Soviet covert biological-weapons programme. See Alibek, *Biohazard: The Chilling True Story of the Largest Covert Biological Weapons Program in the World, Told from the Inside by the Man who Ran It* (New York: Random House, 1999).

25 Amatzia Baram, 'An Analysis of Iraqi WMD Strategy', *The Nonproliferation Review*, vol. 8, no. 2, Summer 2001, pp. 25–39. One scholar has argued that the potential of Iraqi biological attacks against Israel, and the Israeli inclination for a pre-emptive or retaliatory response to such a threat, led to the successful deterrence of an Allied invasion of Baghdad. See Avigdor Haselkorn, *The Continuing Storm: Iraq, Poisonous Weapons, and Deterrence* (New Haven, CT: Yale University Press, 1999).

26 While no White House fact sheet was presented on the DCI, Aspin's remarks have been posted on the Federation of American Scientists' website: http://www.fas.org/irp/offdocs/pdd18.htm.

27 Schneider, *Future War and Counterproliferation*, p. 46.

28 Cited in Philip C. Saunders, 'Military Options for Dealing with North Korea's Nuclear Program', Center for Nonproliferation Studies, 7 January 2003: http://cns.miis.edu/research/korea/dprkmil.htm#fn9.

29 For more on military scenarios involving North Korea, see Michael O'Hanlon, 'Stopping a North Korean Invasion: Why Defending South Korea is Easier than the Pentagon Thinks', *International Security*, vol. 22, no. 4, Spring 1998, pp. 135–70; and Scott Stossel, 'North Korea: The War Game', *The Atlantic Monthly*, vol. 296, no. 1, July/August 2005, pp. 97–108. For a more detailed account of the 1994 North Korea crisis, see Michael J. Mazarr, *North Korea and the Bomb: A Case Study in Non-*

proliferation (New York: St Martin's Press, 1995).

30 Martha Clark, *A False Sense of Security: The Role of Missile Defenses in Counterproliferation Doctrine* (Washington DC: Physicians for Social Responsibility, 2003), p. 18. For a more recent examination of CONPAN-0400, see William Arkin, 'Military is conducting a highly classified Granite Shadow', *The Washington Post*, 21 September 2005.

31 An additional $3bn would be allocated to a technology programme, with potential benefits applicable to both programmes. The BUR's total missile-defence budget was far less than its predecessor's planned $39bn budget. Not surprisingly, while the NMD component was allowed to continue in a much-reduced form, the TMD component's development schedules were not disrupted. See Missile Defense Agency Historian's Office, 'Ballistic Missile Defense: A Brief History': http://www.mda.mil/mdalink/html/briefhis.html.

32 Commission to Assess the Ballistic Missile Threat to the United States, 'Executive Summary', *Report of the Commission to Assess the Ballistic Missile Threat to the United States*, 18 July 1999: http://www.fas.org/irp/threat/bm-threat.htm. This report departed sharply from the traditional intelligence community's assessment of the ballistic-missile threat. The November 1995 National Intelligence Estimate (NIE) predicted that a threat to the US would not take place for at least 15 years. With the recent *unsuccessful* test of North Korea's *Taepodong*-2 ICBM on 4 July 2006, it appears that the NIE estimate remains a far more realistic estimation of the ICBM threat.

33 Robert Shuey, 'Theater Missile Defense: Issues for Congress', *Congressional Research Service (CRS) Issue Brief*, 22 May 2001, p. 2.

34 JCS, *Joint Doctrine for Operations in Nuclear, Biological, or Chemical (NBC) Environments* (Joint Pub 3-11), 11 July 2000, p. I-7 (emphasis added).

35 Cited in Sagan, 'The Commitment Trap: Why the United States Should Not Use Nuclear Threats to Deter Biological and Chemical Weapons Attacks', *International Security*, vol. 24, no. 4, Spring 2000, p. 85.

36 *Ibid.*, p. 93. This threat was supported by the deployment of nuclear weapons to the region. See Stephen I. Schwartz, 'Miscalculated Ambiguity: US Policy on the Use and the Threat of Use of Nuclear Weapons', *Disarmament Diplomacy*, no. 23, February 1998. Such calculated ambiguity was also shown during the more recent 2003 Iraq War, where senior US officials downplayed the possible retaliatory use of nuclear weapons but did not foreswear nuclear retaliation in the event of an Iraqi CB attack. See Wade Boese, 'US Issued Warning on Threat of Possible Iraqi WMD Use', *Arms Control Today*, vol. 33, no. 4, May 2003.

37 This figure is cited in Kristensen, 'Nuclear Futures: Proliferation of Weapons of Mass Destruction and US Nuclear Strategy', *British American Security Information Council Research Report* (February 1998), p. 9.

38 See Kristensen and Handler, 'The USA and Counter-Proliferation', pp. 387–99. The reduction in post-Cold War targets was aided by the interest of General Lee Butler, head of STRATCOM, in attacking nodal networks rather than individual targets. See Kristensen, *US Nuclear Strategy Reform in the 1990s*, Working Paper (Berkeley, CA: The Nautilus Institute, March 2000), p. 4.

39 Kristensen and Handler, 'The USA and Counter-Proliferation', p. 389. One upgrade identified was the MILSTAR/SCOTT satellite communication systems.

40 See Arkin, 'Agnosticism When Real Values are Needed: Nuclear Policy in the Clinton Administration', *Federation of American Scientists Public Interest Report*, vol. 47, no. 5, September–October 1994.

41 *Doctrine for Joint Nuclear Operations*, Joint Pub 3-12 (Washington DC: JCS, 29 April 1993), pp. I-3–I-4.

42 An analysis of each of these studies and briefings can be found in Kristensen, *The Matrix of Deterrence: US Strategic Command Force Structure Studies* (Berkeley, CA: The Nautilus Institute, May 2001), pp. 1–23.

43 See Thomas Dowler and Joseph Howard II, 'Countering the Threat of the Well-Armed Tyrant: A Modest Proposal for Small Nuclear Weapons', *Strategic Review*, Fall 1991. The authors were scientists from Los Alamos National Laboratory, New Mexico.

44 See Arkin, 'Agnosticism When Real Values are Needed'; Arkin, 'Nuclear Junkies: Those lovable little bombs', *Bulletin of the Atomic Scientists*, vol. 49, no. 6, July/August 1993, pp. 22–7.

45 Kristensen, 'Nuclear Futures', p. 14. Primary documents from the counter-proliferation working group and a summary of the group's views, can be found on the Nautilus website: http://nautilus.org/archives/nukestrat/USA/Npr/WG5.html.

46 *Ibid.*, p. 15.

47 See STRATCOM, 'Essentials of Post-Cold War Nuclear Deterrence': http://www.nukestrat.com/us/stratcom/sagessentials.htm.

48 Robert S. Norris and Arkin, 'US nuclear forces, 2000', *Bulletin of the Atomic Scientists*, vol. 56, no. 3, May/June 2000, pp. 69–71.

49 For more on this weapon, see Greg Mello, 'New Bomb, New Mission', *Bulletin of the Atomic Scientists*, vol. 52, no. 3, May/June 1997, pp. 28–32

50 Kristensen, *US Nuclear Strategy Reform in the 1990s*, p. 5.

51 Kristensen, 'Nuclear Futures', p. 12; Kristensen, 'Nuclear Mission Creep: The Impact of Weapons of Mass Destruction Proliferation on US Nuclear Policy and Planning', Presentation to The Program on Science and Global Security, Princeton University, 11 May 2005: http://www.nukestrat.com/pubs/Brief2005_Princeton.pdf.

Chapter Three

1 *Nuclear Posture Review [Excerpts]*, p. 1.

2 This would most logically support the offensive and defensive legs of the new triad. Interestingly, then Principal Deputy Under Secretary of Defense for Policy Stephen Cambone appears to have supported having the C^2I system, rather than a revitalised defence infrastructure, as the third leg of the new triad. This anecdote is recounted in Dr Jeffrey Lewis's blog: at http://www.armscontrolwonk.com/900/new-triad-2-cambone-on-the-new-triad.

3 See Payne (study director), *Rationale and Requirements for US Nuclear Forces and Arms Control, Vol. I: Executive Report* (Fairfax, VA: National Institute for Public Policy, January 2001). Many of the participants of this study would go on to hold key positions in the Bush administration, including Ambassador Linton S. Brooks, Dr Stephen Cambone, Payne, Stephen J. Hadley, Dr William J. Schneider Jr and Ambassador Robert Joseph.

4 *Quadrennial Defense Review Report* (Washington DC: DoD, 30 September 2001), p. 14.

5 *Nuclear Posture Review [Excerpts]*, p. 7.

6 *Ibid.*, p. 16.

7 This is from the classified version of NSPD-17, as cited in Kralev, 'Bush Signs Paper Allowing Nuclear Response'.

8 Jason D. Ellis, '"The Gravest Danger": Proliferation, Terrorism, and the Bush Doctrine', *The Monitor*, vol. 9, no. 1, Winter/Spring 2003, p. 5.

9 *The National Security Strategy of the United States* (Washington DC: The White House, September 2002), p. 14. Bush's 2002 State of the Union address is also noteworthy, in the fact that the president uses the term 'Axis of Evil' to target Iraq, Iran and North Korea specifically.

[10] According to the NPR, the new triad will contribute to four defence-policy goals: assure, dissuade, deter, defeat. See *Nuclear Posture Review [Excerpts]*, pp. 12–14. The need to defeat potential adversaries is so prevalent that some critics have argued that an implicit goal of the new triad is the nuclear *pre-emption* of potential adversaries. For example, see Roger Speed and Michael May, 'Dangerous Doctrine', *Bulletin of the Atomic Scientists*, vol. 61, no. 2, March/April 2005, pp. 38–49. However, it would be a mistake to conclude that pre-emption is indeed a goal of the NPR. After all, it does not explicitly advocate the pre-emptive use of these weapons (as compared to the explicit pre-emptive/preventive doctrine enshrined in the 2002 NSS). In addition, nuclear pre-emption has never been eliminated from American or NATO nuclear-war plans.

[11] *Nuclear Posture Review [Excerpts]*, pp. 12–13.

[12] See Norris and Kristensen, 'US nuclear forces, 2006', *Bulletin of the Atomic Scientists*, vol. 62, no. 1, January/February 2006, pp. 68–71.

[13] *Quadrennial Defense Review Report* (Washington DC: DoD, 6 February 2006), p. 50.

[14] Wade Boese, 'Bush Plans to Cut Atomic Arsenal', *Arms Control Today*, vol. 34, no. 6, July/August 2004.

[15] For more on the difficulty of destroying Russian silos, see *The US Nuclear War Plan: a Time for Change* (New York: National Resources Defense Council, June 2001), ch. 3.

[16] See Adam J. Hebert, 'The Future Missile Force', *Air Force Magazine*, vol. 86, no. 10, October 2003, pp. 64–8. There are some conflicting reports on the current status of the *Minuteman* Elite concept. The Air Force Space Command (AFSP) analysis of alternatives appears to have rejected it. However, General Lance Lord, the head of AFSP, has recently noted that the command remains interested in this concept. See Hebert, 'The ICBM Makeover', *Air Force Magazine*, vol. 88, no. 10, October 2005, pp. 34–9 and British American Security Intelligence Council, Washington Nuclear Update, 8 March 2006: http://www.basicint.org/update/WNU060308.htm#0108.

[17] Depressed trajectories feature more difficult atmospheric re-entry. The use of a MARV would allow modifications to the re-entry configuration and, therefore, eliminate one of the problems associated with depressed trajectories. See McDonough, 'The US Nuclear Shift to the Pacific: Implications for "Strategic Stability"', *RUSI Journal*, vol. 151, no. 2, April 2006, pp. 64–68. For more on depressed trajectories, see Lisbeth Gronlund and David C. Wright, 'Depressed trajectory SLBMs: A Technical Evaluation and Arms Control Possibilities', *Science & Global Security*, vol. 3, no. 1–2, 1992, pp. 101–59.

[18] The US strategic modernisation programmes are detailed in Norris and Kristensen, 'US nuclear forces, 2006', pp. 68–71. For more on the stalled B-52 bomber reductions, see John A. Tirpak, 'The New Air Force Program', *Air Force Magazine*, vol. 89, no. 7, July 2006, pp. 30–36.

[19] *Report to Congress on the Defeat of Hardened and Deeply Buried Targets* (Washington DC: Department of Energy and Defense, July 2001), p. 8. Previously, American concerns over these targets had led to 'mission-needs' statements for an HDBT defeat capability by STRATCOM and Combat Air Forces in 1994 and the *Project Sand Dune* study on the utility of a nuclear HDBT capability in 1997.

[20] The 10,000 HDBT estimate is from the *Defense Science Board Task Force on Underground Facilities*, which is cited in *Nuclear Posture Review [Excerpts]*, p. 46. For more on different types of HDBTs, see Michael A. Levi, *Fire in the Hole: Nuclear and Non-nuclear Options for Counter-Proliferation*, Carnegie Paper no. 31, (Washington DC: Carnegie Endowment for International Peace, November 2002). The full text is available to download from: http://www.carnegieendowment.

org/publications/index.cfm?fa=view&id=1115&prog=zgp&proj=znpp.

21 *HDBT Report*, p. 9.

22 For more on the platform attributes to destroy MRTs, see Christopher J. Bowie, *Destroying Mobile Ground Targets in an Anti-Access Environment*, Analysis Center Papers (Washington DC: Northrop Grumman's Analysis Center, December 2001): http://www.analysiscenter.northropgrumman.com/files/mobile_ground_targets.pdf.

23 See Glaser and Fetter, 'Counterforce Revisited', pp. 96–7.

24 See Levi, *Fire in the Hole*, pp. 17–21.

25 See the BLU-116 Advanced Unitary Penetrator factsheet on the Globalsecurity.org website: http://www.globalsecurity.org/military/systems/munitions/blu-116.htm.

26 See Levi, *Fire in the Hole*, pp. 24–25; *HDBT Report*, p. 24.

27 The use of conventional ballistic-missile delivery systems also promises to increase the potential speed and, therefore, the kinetic-kill capabilities of earth penetrators. The US has also been looking at the potential development of conventional ICBMs, which can either be based on the deactivated MX ICBM force or the limited number of soon-to-be deactivated *Minuteman* III ICBMs, as well as conventional (and stealthy) ACMs for the intercontinental bomber force. For more on the possibility of a conventional ICBM force, see *Report of the Defense Science Board Task Force on the Future of Strategic Strike Forces* (Washington DC: Defense Science Board, February 2004), pp. 5-1–5-16.

28 *Nuclear Posture Review [Excerpts]*, p. 1.

29 *Ibid.*, p. 47.

30 *HDBT Report*, p. 19.

31 *Nuclear Posture Review [Excerpts]*, p. 47.

32 Norris, Kristensen, and Christopher E. Paine, *Nuclear Insecurity: A Critique of the Bush Administration's Nuclear Weapons Policies* (New York: National Resources Defense Council, September 2004), p. 11: http://www.nrdc.org/nuclear/insecurity/critique.pdf.

33 Cited in Kristensen, *Global Strike: A Chronology of the Pentagon's New Offensive Strike Plan* (Washington DC: Federation of American Scientists, March 2006), p. 4: http://www.fas.org/ssp/docs/GlobalStrikeReport.pdf.

34 See Arkin, 'Not Just a Last Resort?', *Washington Post*, 15 May 2005, p. B01. See also Kristensen, *Global Strike*, pp. 3–11.

35 Under Unified Command Plan Change 2, STRATCOM was assigned four missions: (i) global missile defence; (ii) global strike, or the ability to hit any target on earth quickly; (iii) DoD Information Operations; and (iv) command, control, communications, computers, intelligence, surveillance and reconnaissance. This was followed in March 2005 with the assignment of a fifth mission, combating WMD, which represents the culmination of STRATCOM's long-standing efforts to become the lead command for counter-proliferation. Despite the expansion of missions, STRATCOM's traditional mission of strategic deterrence – with responsibilities for the planning, targeting and employment of nuclear weapons – is unique to the command and remains separated from conventional missions.

36 NSPD-23, *National Policy on Ballistic Missile Defense* (Washington DC: The White House, 16 December 2002). NSPD-23 remains classified, but was leaked to Bill Gertz at *The Washington Times*, and is available at: http://www.fas.org/irp/offdocs/nspd/nspd-23.htm. The White House did release an unclassified 'fact sheet' of NSPD-23 on 20 May 2003, with some passages omitted, which can be found at: http://www.fas.org/irp/offdocs/nspd/nspd-23-fs.htm.

37 *Nuclear Posture Review [Excerpts]*, p. 2. The need for such an insurance policy stems from the long-standing American discomfort over its societal vulnerability to nuclear weapons and its suspicion of relying solely on offensive nuclear deterrence to deal with this vulnerability.

38 JCS, *Department of Defense Dictionary of Military and Associated Terms* (Joint Pub

1-02), 12 April 2001, amended through 14 April 2006, p. 403.

39 The current threat environment is fixated on the dangers of CB agents, against which passive defence measures can – in contrast to even a rudimentary fission weapon – be more feasibly employed. See Betts, 'The New Threat of Mass Destruction', *Foreign Affairs*, vol. 77, no. 1, January–February 1998, pp. 26–41.

40 *DoD Dictionary*, p. 4.

41 Bush, 'Remarks by the President to Students and Faculty at National Defense University', Office of the Press Secretary, 1 May 2001: http://www.whitehouse.gov/news/releases/2001/05/20010501-10.html.

42 See NSPD-23, *National Policy on BMD*. As NSPD-23 notes, 'some of the systems we are pursuing, such as boost-phase defenses, are intended to be capable of intercepting missiles of all ranges, blurring the distinction between theater and national missile defenses'.

43 For more on a multi-layered approach to missile defense, see Steven A. Hildrath (coordinator), 'Missile Defense: A Debate', *CRS Report to Congress*, 19 July 2005, esp. pp. 11–13.

44 For more on these acquisition models, see Philip Coyle, 'Rhetoric or Reality? Missile Defense Under Bush', *Arms Control Today*, vol. 32, no. 4, May 2002. This represents the repudiation of what has been termed the 'Nitze deployment criteria', which advocated that defences should only be developed if deployments were effective, survivable and cost-effective at the margin (vis-à-vis offensive deployments). These criteria were first introduced in a speech by Paul H. Nitze and codified in the Reagan administration's NNDD-172, and would form the basis for the Clinton administration's own NMD criteria.

45 Boese, 'Pentagon Seeks Missile Defense Budget Increase, Reorganization', *Arms Control Today*, vol. 31, no. 6, July/August 2001.

46 Gronlund and Wright, 'The Alaska Test Bed Fallacy: Missile Defense Deployment Goes Stealth', *Arms Control Today*, vol. 31, no. 7, September 2001.

47 *Nuclear Posture Review [Excerpts]*, p. 26.

48 *Ibid.*

49 See NSPD-23, *National Policy on BMD.*

50 See Boese, 'Missile defense funding soars to new heights', *Arms Control Today*, vol. 36, no. 2, March 2006; Boese, 'Defense Bills Passed; Nuclear Questions Raised', *Arms Control Today*, vol. 36, no. 1, January/February 2006; Boese, 'Hill Passes Defense Authorization Bill', *Arms Control Today*, vol. 34, no. 9, November 2004; Boese, 'Congress Grants Administration $9.1 Billion for Missile Defense', *Arms Control Today*, vol. 33, no. 8, October 2003; and Boese, 'Congress Authorizes 2003 Missile Defense Funding', *Arms Control Today*, vol. 32, no. 10, December 2002.

51 Boese, 'Ship-Based Anti-Missile System Scores Hit', *Arms Control Today*, vol. 35, no. 10, December 2005.

52 Boese, 'Missile defense funding soars to new heights'.

53 If an American missile-defence shield becomes operational prior to a BMD shield for European and potentially other allies, a 'window of vulnerability' could develop whereby allies – but not the United States – would be vulnerable to WMD blackmail. This could have profound implications for American security guarantees to these allies, and could represent the first step towards American strategic disengagement from European security. For more on this issue, see James Fergusson, 'The Coupling Paradox: Nuclear Weapons, Ballistic Missile Defense, and the Future of the Transatlantic Relationship', in Alexander Moens, Lenard J. Cohen, and Allen G. Sens, eds, *NATO and European Security: Alliance Politics from the End of the Cold War to the Age of Terrorism* (Westport, CT: Praeger, 2003), pp. 153–72.

54 For an overview of these various programmes, see Hildrath, 'Missile Defense: A Debate'. The other element of the SBIRS programme, namely the SBIRS-High project, is meant to field a replacement to the current Defense Support Program

space-based launch detection system. Its capability is relevant to missile defence, but due to its wider function it is under the Air Force's jurisdiction. However, this programme also has similar problems as the STSS.

55 James M. Lindsay and Michael O'Hanlon, 'Missile Defense after the ABM Treaty', *The Washington Quarterly*, vol. 25, no. 3, Summer 2002, p. 165.

56 Kurt Guthe, 'The Nuclear Posture Review: How Is the "New Triad" New?', (Washington DC: Center for Strategic and Budgetary Assessments, August 2002), p. 6.

57 *Nuclear Posture Review [Excerpts]*, p. 3.

58 Jonathan Medalia, 'Nuclear Weapons: The Reliable Replacement Warhead Program', *CRS Report to Congress*, 9 March 2006.

59 *Nuclear Posture Review [Excerpts]*, p. 30.

60 Christine Kucia, 'US Produces First Plutonium Pit Since 1989', *Arms Control Today*, vol. 33, no. 4, May 2003.

61 See Jace Radke, 'Defense Official: Nuke Tests at NTS Are Likely', *Las Vegas Times*, 14 August 2002; Dan Stober and Jonathan Landay, 'US ponders resumption of nuclear weapons tests', *The San Jose Mercury News*, 16 November 2002, p. A17. The Aldridge memo can be found at: http://www.lasg.org/technical/NuclearWeaponsCouncilMemo.pdf. The memo was followed by a 10 January meeting of significant nuclear-weapons managers to plan for a NWC 'Stockpile Stewardship Conference'. The notes of the meeting, which were obtained by the Los Alamos Study Group, indicates a desire to study the need to make testing modifications in order to build the new kinds of nuclear weapons advocated in the NPR. The minutes of the meeting can be found at: http://www.lasg.org/technical/press-smallnukes.htm.

62 Other facilities under development as part of the SSP include the National Ignition Facility, the Dual Axis Radiographic Hydrotest Facility and pulse-power technology facilities. These data, alongside data from subcritical tests, are planned to be integrated through the Accelerated Strategic Computing Initiative, a multi-billion-dollar super-computing programme incorporating leading universities in the United States.

63 See Boese, 'Warhead Initiative Looms Large in NNSA Plans', *Arms Control Today*, vol. 36, no. 2, March 2006; Boese, 'Congress Cuts Nuclear Bunker Buster Again', *Arms Control Today*, vol. 35, no. 10, December 2005; Boese, 'Congress Axes Funding for New Nukes', *Arms Control Today*, vol. 34, no. 10, December 2004; and Christine Kucia, 'Congress Authorizes New Weapons Research', *Arms Control Today*, vol. 33, no. 10, December 2003.

64 *Nuclear Posture Review [Excerpts]*, pp. 34–5.

65 Medalia, 'Nuclear Weapon Initiatives: Low-yield R&D, Advanced Concepts, Earth Penetrators, Test Readiness', *CRS Report to Congress*, 8 March 2004, p. 26.

66 See Medalia, '"Bunker Busters": Robust Nuclear Earth Penetrator Issues FY2005–FY2007', *CRS Report to Congress*, 21 February 2006 and Medalia, 'Nuclear Weapon Initiatives'. Also see Boese, 'US Weighing Nuclear Stockpile Changes', *Arms Control Today* vol. 35, no. 4, May 2005 and Boese, 'Warhead Initiative Looms Large in NNSA Plans'.

67 See K. Henry O'Brien, Bryan L. Fearey, Michael R. Sjulin and Greg A. Thomas, *Sustaining the Nuclear Enterprise: a New Approach, UCRL-AR-212442, LAUR-05-3830, SAND2005-3384* (Lawrence Livermore National Laboratory, Los Alamos National Laboratory and Sandia National Laboratories, 20 May 2005): http://www.nukewatch.org/facts/nwd/SustainingtheEnterprise.pdf#search=%22Bruce%20T.%20Goodwin%20Sustaining%20the%20Nuclear%20Enterprise%3A%20%E2%80%94a%20New%20Approach%22.

68 Daryl G. Kimball, 'Replacement Nuclear Warheads? Buyer Beware', *Arms Control Today*, vol. 35, no. 4, May 2005. Also see William J. Broad, 'US Redesigning Atomic

Weapons', *New York Times*, 27 February 2005.

69 See Nuclear Weapons Complex Infrastructure Task Force, *Recommendations for the Nuclear Weapons Complex of the Future* (Secretary of Energy Advisory Board, US Department of Energy, 13 July 2005).

Chapter Four

1 *Nuclear Posture Review [Excerpts]*, p. 13.

2 Bush, 'Remarks by the President at 2002 Graduation Exercise of the United States Military Academy', Office of the Press Secretary, 1 June 2002. The 2002 NSS would use the phrase 'we must build and maintain our defenses beyond challenge'. *National Security Strategy*, p. 29. For more on the revolutionary nature of the Bush administration's strategy, see Gaddis, 'A Grand Strategy of Transformation', *Foreign Policy*, no. 133, November/December 2002, pp. 50–57.

3 Posen, 'Command of the Commons: The Military Foundation of US Hegemony', *International Security*, vol. 28, no. 1, Summer 2003, p. 6. For more on the post-Cold War debate on American grand-strategy options, see Posen and Andrew L. Ross, 'Competing Visions for US Grand Strategy', pp. 5–53; Douglas A. Ross and Christopher N.B. Ross, 'From "Neo-Isolationism" to "Imperial Liberalism": "Grand Strategy" Options in the American International Security Debate and the Implications for Canada', in McDonough and Douglas A. Ross, eds, *The Dilemmas of American Strategic Primacy: Implications for the Future of Canadian–American Cooperation* (Toronto, ON: Royal Canadian Military Institute, 2005), pp. 165–217.

4 For more on 'imperial overreach', see Graham E. Fuller, 'Strategic fatigue', *The National Interest*, vol. 84, Summer 2006, pp. 37–42. Primacy may have been the strategy of choice for Republican neo-conservatives, but it was also an element of the Clinton administration's own policies that became, under the leadership of more hawkish Democrats, such as then-Secretary of State Madeleine Albright and diplomat Richard Holbrooke, progressively stronger in Clinton's second term. These 'national security Democrats', a term introduced by Holbrooke, now dominate the perceived Democratic front-runners for the presidential nomination in 2008 (including Senators Joseph Biden and Hillary Clinton). For more on this trend, see Jeffrey Goldberg, 'The Unbranding', *The New Yorker*, 21 March 2005 and Ari Berman, 'The Strategic Class', *The Nation*, 29 August 2005.

5 The Defense Special Weapons Agency noted that the international environment had changed from a 'weapons-rich environment' into a 'target-rich environment'. Kristensen, 'Targets of Opportunity', pp. 22–8.

6 Wade L. Huntley, 'Threats all the way down: US strategic initiatives in a unipolar world', *Review of International Studies*, vol. 32, no. 1, January 2006, p. 64.

7 See Frank Harvey, 'The future of strategic stability and nuclear deterrence', *International Journal*, vol. 58, no. 2, Spring 2003, pp. 321–46. For more on the second nuclear age, see Paul Bracken, 'The Second Nuclear Age', pp. 146–56 and Gray, *The Second Nuclear Age* (Boulder, CO: Lynne Rienner, 1999).

8 Betts, 'The New Threat of Mass Destruction', p. 31.

9 See Edward Rhodes, 'Conventional Deterrence', *Comparative Strategy*, vol. 19, no. 3, July–September 2000, pp. 221–53.

10 See Charles L. Glaser and Steve Fetter, 'Counterforce Revisited: Assessing the Nuclear Posture Review's New Missions', *International Security*, vol. 30, no. 2, Fall 2005, p. 103.

11 Robert E. Harkavy, 'Triangular or Indirect Deterrence/Compellence: Something

New in Deterrence Theory', *Comparative Strategy*, vol. 17, no. 1, January–March 1998, p. 64.

12 This point is reiterated in Paul Bracken, 'The Second Nuclear Age', *Foreign Affairs*, vol. 79, no. 1, January/February 2000, pp. 146–56.

13 For a critical examination of American resolve during scenarios of regional deterrence, see Dean Wilkening and Kenneth Watman, *Nuclear Deterrence in a Regional Context* (Santa Monica, CA: RAND, 1995), ch. 1.

14 Gray, 'Deterrence and Regional Conflicts: Hopes, Fallacies, and Fixes', *Comparative Strategy*, vol. 17, no. 1, January–March 1998, p. 57.

15 For more on the problems with deterring rogue states in the post-Cold War period, see Payne, *Deterrence in the Second Nuclear Age*, esp. ch. 2.

16 Glaser and Fetter, 'Counterforce Revisited', p. 53.

17 For a recent example, see Seymour Hersh, 'The Iran Plans', *The New Yorker*, 17 April 2006.

18 Scenarios that are used include: an adversary intending to use WMD against American forces or allies; imminent attack from an adversary's biological-weapon capabilities; attacks on facilities (HDBTs, C^3) that are required for an adversary to execute a WMD attack; and to demonstrate US intent and capability to use nuclear weapons as a tool of deterrence. See JCS, *Doctrine for Joint Nuclear Operations* (Joint Pub 3-12), Final Coordination [2] Draft, 15 March 2005: http://www.nukestrat.com/us/jcs/JCS_JP3-12_05draft.pdf. This document, the contents of which were highlighted in *Arms Control Today* and the *Washington Post*, would later be removed from the Pentagon website and cancelled. Also see Kristensen, 'The Role of Nuclear Weapons: New Doctrine Falls Short of Bush Pledge', *Arms Control Today*, vol. 35, no. 7, September 2005.

19 *Doctrine for Joint Nuclear Operations*, p. II-10.

20 See Ball and Toth, 'Revising the SIOP', pp. 75–6.

21 Bruce Blair, 'We Keep Buiding Nukes for All the Wrong Reasons', *Washington Post*, 25 May 2003: http://www.cdi.org/blair/new-nukes.cfm.

22 See Glaser and Fetter, 'Counterforce Revisited', pp. 96–7.

23 Cirincione, 'A Deeply Flawed Review', Testimony before the Senate Foreign Relations Committee, 16 May 2002: http://www.carnegieendowment.org/publications/index.cfm?fa=view&id=988. For another sceptical perspective, see Richard Sokolsky, 'Demystifying the US Nuclear Posture Review', *Survival*, vol. 44, no. 3, Autumn 2002, pp. 133–48.

24 Lieber and Press, 'The End of MAD? The Nuclear Dimension of US Primacy', *International Security*, vol. 30, no. 4, Spring 2006, p. 30.

25 Such an approach would also have the benefit of minimising the impact on Russian or Chinese threat perceptions. TMDs can be tailored not to affect a country's nuclear deterrent either, while a thin area defence could be easily saturated and might even be used as a means of protecting retaliatory forces and C^3 systems, which would further assure a second-strike capability. See Glaser and Fetter, 'National Missile Defense and the Future of US Nuclear Weapons Policy', *International Security*, vol. 26, no. 1, Summer 2001, pp. 40–92 and Douglas A. Ross, 'American Missile Defence, Grand Strategy and Global Security', in McDonough and Ross, eds, *The Dilemmas of American Strategic Primacy*, pp. 35–66.

26 See Glaser, 'Nuclear Policy without an Adversary: US Planning for the Post-Soviet Era', *International Security*, vol. 16, no. 4, Spring 1992, pp. 34–78. For a compatible and nuanced perspective of MAD, see Jervis, *The Meaning of the Nuclear Revolution: Statecraft and the Prospects of Armageddon* (Ithaca, NY: Cornell University Press, 1989), esp. ch. 3.

27 For more on arms racing and the potential for sub-optimal outcomes, see Glaser,

'When Are Arms Races Dangerous? Rational vs. Suboptimal Arming', *International Security*, vol. 28, no. 4, Spring 2004, pp. 44–84.

28 Glaser, 'Nuclear Policy without an Adversary', p. 41.

29 A counter-force second-strike capability was rationalised by the need to have accurate and high-yield counter-force weapons that would be both survivable against a Soviet first strike and capable of neutralising the Soviet reserve force. This would prevent the Nitze scenario's fears of a Soviet advantage in the ratio of residual forces. For a nuanced argument for a limited counter-force second-strike capability, see Sagan, *Moving Targets*, ch. 2.

30 See Stephen Fruhling, '"Bunker Busters" and Intra-War Deterrence: A Case for Caution and Two Solutions', *Comparative Strategy*, vol. 24, no. 4, October/November 2005, pp. 327–341.

31 See Payne, *Deterrence in the Second Nuclear Age*, ch. 4.

32 The Nitze deployment criteria were difficult to meet against the Soviet Union, but it is certainly much more questionable whether rogue states would have sufficient technological capability or resources to initiate sufficient off-setting countermeasures and defence-suppression capabilities. As such, defensive deployments would be much more rational and justified against rogue states as opposed to a potential major-power adversary.

33 Glaser and Fetter, 'Counterforce Revisited', p. 86. This is, of course, dependent on the successful development of nuclear EPWs. See Robert W. Nelson, 'Low-Yield Earth-Penetrating Nuclear Weapons', *Science and Global Security*, vol. 10, no. 1, January 2002, pp. 1–20

34 See Glaser and Fetter, 'Counterforce Revisited', p. 112.

35 See Baram, 'An Analysis of Iraq's WMD Strategy', pp. 25–39 and 'The Commitment Trap', pp. 107–10. For more on the 'fail-deadly' dangers posed by a 'delegative' command-and-control system, see Peter D. Feaver, 'Command and Control in Emerging Nuclear Nations', *International Security*, vol. 17, no. 3, Winter 1992–1993, pp. 160–87. For an interesting examination of Iraqi deterrent options in the run-up to the 2003 Iraq War, see Avigdor Haselkorn, 'Iraq's Biowarfare Options: Last Resort, Preemption, or a Blackmail Option?', *Biosecurity and Bioterrorism*, vol. 1, no. 1, March 2003, pp. 19–26.

36 See Feaver, 'Command and Control', pp. 160–87 and Sagan, 'The Perils of Proliferation', pp. 66–107. For a neo-optimist perspective, see David J. Karl, 'Proliferation Pessimism and Emerging Nuclear Powers', *International Security*, vol. 21, no. 3, Winter 1996/97, pp. 87–119.

37 Cruise missiles have a number of advantages compared to ballistic missiles or aircraft. For example, the delivery platforms use relatively low-cost and widespread technology, have significant advantages against either air defence or any future workable missile-defence system and would be compact enough to be forward deployed in a commercial ship. Moreover, the aerodynamic stability and low-flying trajectory of cruise missiles makes these weapons a far more reliable means of storing and disseminating CB agents. See Dennis M. Gormley, 'Cruise Control', *The Bulletin of the Atomic Scientists*, vol. 62, no. 2, March/April 2006, pp. 26–33 and Col Rex R. Kiziah, 'The Emerging Biocruise Threat', *Air and Space Power Journal*, vol. 17, no. 1, Spring 2003, pp. 81–94.

38 Prepositioned WMD may be a high-risk strategy, given the possible consequences of being caught. But if multiple WMD devices could be successfully prepositioned in the United States, especially strategic capabilities such as nuclear devices and biological agents with effective dissemination systems, a rogue state would be in a far stronger position for coercion. Such capabilities would be invulnerable to counterforce and/or decapitation attacks and would be exceedingly difficult to locate and neutralise. It would also be impossible to know fully the total number

of prepositioned devices. A rogue state could thereby undertake a limited demonstration attack and threaten sequential attacks in the event that its demands are not met. See Stan Erickson, 'Nuclear Weapon Prepositioning as a Threat Strategy', *Journal of Homeland Security*, July 2001:http://www.homelandsecurity.org/journal/articles/Erickson.html.

39 See Lieber and Press, 'The End of MAD?' pp. 7–44.

40 See Jeffrey Lewis, 'The Ambiguous Arsenal', *The Bulletin of the Atomic Scientists*, vol. 61, no. 3, May/June 2005, pp. 52–9 and Norris and Kristensen, 'Chinese nuclear forces, 2006', *The Bulletin of the Atomic Scientists*, vol. 62, no. 3, May/June 2006, pp. 60–63.

41 See McDonough, 'The US Nuclear Shift to the Pacific', pp. 64–8.

42 The deployment of TMD systems in the Pacific, especially sea-based systems in the context of joint US–Japan development, would also be seen as possibly heralding further Japanese remilitarisation, e.g. a 'shield' to protect the Japanese 'sword', and the deployment of an area-defence capability for Taiwan. See Thomas J. Christensen, 'China, the US–Japan Alliance, and the Security Dilemma in East Asia', *International Security*, vol. 23, no. 4, Spring 1999, pp. 49–80.

43 *Nuclear Posture Review [Excerpts]*, pp. 16–17.

44 For more on escalation dominance in the US–China relationship, see Robert S. Ross, 'Navigating the Taiwan Straits: Deterrence, Escalation Dominance, and US–China Relations', *International Security*, vol. 27, no. 2, Fall 2002, pp. 48–85.

45 Jing-dong Yuan, 'Chinese Response to US Missile Defense: Implications for Arms Control and Regional Security', *The Nonproliferation Review*, vol. 10, no. 1, Spring 2003, p. 88.

46 Douglas A. Ross, 'American Missile Defence, Grand Strategy and Global Security', pp. 44–45. The destruction of these 'soft' targets could potentially neutralise American defensive capabilities and, if based on a conventional pre-emptive attack, could be sufficiently limited so as not to warrant a nuclear response. Such an attack might be seen as a potentially feasible means of obtaining a bargaining advantage during a crisis. Vulnerable missile-defence systems could, therefore, inject a destabilising escalation level in any crisis scenario.

47 See Phillip D. Saunders and Yuan, 'Chinese Strategic Force Modernization: Issues and Implications for the United States', in Michael Barletta, ed., *Proliferation Challenges and Nonproliferation Opportunities for New Administrations*, Occasional Paper No. 4 (Monterey, CA: Center for Nonproliferation Studies, Monterey Institute of International Studies, September 2000), pp. 40–46. For more on limited deterrence, see Alastair Iain Johnston, 'China's New "Old Thinking": The Concept of Limited Deterrence', *International Security*, vol. 20, no. 2, Winter 1995/96, pp. 5–42.

48 Norris and Kristensen, 'Russian nuclear forces, 2006', *The Bulletin of the Atomic Scientists*, vol. 62, no. 2, March/April 2006, pp. 64–7.

49 Lieber and Press, 'The End of MAD?', pp. 7–44. This model is based on a disarming strike against Russia's strategic forces. A decapitation strategy may, however, be even more feasible given the centralised nature of the Soviet C^3 system.

50 For a critique of the Lieber and Press first-strike model, see Valery Yarynich and Steven Starr, '"Nuclear Primacy" is a Fallacy', *Intelligent.ru*:http://english.intelligent.ru/articles/scenarios.htm. This article was originally published in Russian on 26 May 2006 by the Center for Arms Control, Energy and Environmental Studies.

51 Gaps in Russia's early warning radar coverage, particularly the termination of the Yeniseysk (Krasnoyarsk) in the north-east and Skrunda in the northwest, have opened potential 'attack corridors' for American strategic forces. Meanwhile, its

inability to replace '*Oko*' satellite constellations quickly have left US ICBM fields without periodic coverage, while the slow speed of *Prognoz* satellite deployments have prevented crucial warning capability against the lethal American force of SLBMs. See Pavel Podvig, 'History and the Current Status of the Russian Early-Warning System', *Science and Global Security*, vol. 10, no. 1, January 2002, pp. 21–60.

52 Glaser, 'Nuclear Policy Without an Adversary', pp. 42–3.

53 See Norris and Kristensen, 'Russian nuclear forces, 2006', pp. 64–7.

54 This claim is based on Congressional testimony by Col Stanislav Lunev, the highest-ranking GRU military intelligence officer to defect to the United States, and remains uncollaborated. There is, however, evidence that the Soviets did develop tactical 'suitcase' bombs and, according to the former KGB defector Vasili Mitrokhin, special-operations units were active in placing conventional-weapon caches among NATO countries. This lends credibility to the proposition that the Soviets did undertake a nuclear-prepositioning strategy, probably for the decapitation of the American leadership, during the Cold War. See Transcript of the House of Representatives, Committee on National Security, Military Research and Development Subcommittee meeting, 4 August 1998: http://commdocs.house.gov/committees/security/has216010.000/has216010_of.htm; Transcript of the House of Representatives, Committee on Armed Services, Military Research and Development Subcommittee meeting, 26 October 1998: http://www.fas.org/spp/starwars/congress/1999_h/has299010_0.htm.

55 For more on the possibility of accidental or inadvertent nuclear war, see Blair, *Global Zero Alert for Nuclear Forces* (Washington DC: The Brookings Institution, 1995) and David E. Mosher, Lowell H. Schwartz, David R. Howell and Lynn Davis, *Beyond the Nuclear Shadow: A Phased Approach for Improving Nuclear Safety and US–Russian Relations* (Santa Monica, CA: RAND, 2003), ch. 2.

56 The *Perimetr* system is only quasi-automated, as it does require giving preliminary authorisation to a command crew located in a super-hardened facility, who would be able to launch the *Perimetr* command missiles manually. Once launched, however, these missiles would transmit radio signals to the launchers themselves, which would bypass lower command levels in order to launch the ICBM force *automatically*. There is still some debate on whether such a system would be destabilising. For contrasting views, see Blair, 'Russia's Doomsday Machine', *New York Times*, 8 October 1993 and Yarynich, 'The Doomsday Machine's Safety Catch', *New York Times*, 1 February 1994, p. A17. Further information on *Perimetr* can be found in Yarynich, *C3: Nuclear Command, Control and Cooperation* (Washington DC: Center for Defense Information, 2003), ch. 4.

57 Further geostrategic competition would likely stimulate further Russian interest in LUA, especially if its efforts to increase the survivability of its strategic arsenal were successful. This could lead to the development of a fully automated 'dead hand' system that was explored in the 1980s. For more on this system, see Pavel Provlig, 'Dr. Strangelove Meets Reality': http://russianforces.org/blog/2006/04/dr_strangelove_meets_reality.shtml.

Conclusion

1 Ellis, 'The Gravest Danger', pp. 6–7.

2 To borrow from Glaser's argument, nuclear primacy could lead to both a 'sub-optimal' outcome among great powers and a 'rational' outcome – even if potentially destabilising – among rogue states. See Glaser, 'When Are Arms Races Dangerous', pp. 44–84.

3 Territorial boost-phase interception is an especially promising means of strategic defence, in that any interceptors would have to be placed close to the target and could not feasibly threaten all the launch sites of a major power. See Wilkening, 'Airborne Boost-phase Ballistic Missile Defense', *Science and Global Security*, vol. 12, no. 1–2, January–August 2004, pp. 1–67.

4 It is more debatable whether new low-yield weapons would provide any militarily useful deterrent capability aside from their usability. Any strategically vital HDBTs that conventional counterforce weapons are unable to neutralise will, more than likely, require high-yield nuclear warheads for their neutralisation. Low-yield weapons would, moreover, still have too large a radius of destruction to be feasibly employed as ADWs. See Glaser and Fetter, 'Counterforce Revisited', pp. 84–126.

5 This posture is similar to Sagan's argument for a 'second-strike counterforce' posture. See Sagan, *Moving Targets*, ch. 2.

6 See George Bunn and Roland M. Timerbaev, 'Security Assurances to Non-Nuclear-Weapon States', *The Nonproliferation Review*, vol. 1, no. 1, Fall 1993, pp. 11–21; Bunn, 'The Legal Status of US Negative Security Assurances to Non-Nuclear Weapon States', *The Nonproliferation Review*, vol. 4, no. 3, Spring–Summer 1997, pp. 1–17.

For Product Safety Concerns and Information please contact our EU representative GPSR@taylorandfrancis.com
Taylor & Francis Verlag GmbH, Kaufingerstraße 24, 80331 München, Germany

www.ingramcontent.com/pod-product-compliance
Lightning Source LLC
Chambersburg PA
CBHW052131010526
44113CB00034B/1752
* 9 7 8 0 4 1 5 4 2 7 3 4 0 *